# PRINCIPLES OF EDUCATION

## FOR

## TEACHERS IN AFRICA

# PRINCIPLES OF EDUCATION
# FOR
# TEACHERS IN AFRICA

### E. B. CASTLE

*Formerly Professor of Education and Director of the Institute of Education in the University of Hull. Visiting Professor at Makerere University College, Uganda, 1961–1965*

**NAIROBI**
**OXFORD UNIVERSITY PRESS**
OXFORD  NEW YORK

Oxford University Press

OXFORD LONDON GLASGOW
NEW YORK TORONTO MELBOURNE WELLINGTON
NAIROBI DAR ES SALAAM CAPE TOWN
KUALA LUMPUR SINGAPORE HONG KONG TOKYO
DELHI BOMBAY CALCUTTA MADRAS KARACHI

*Oxford University Press, P.O. Box 72532, Nairobi, Kenya*

ISBN 0 19 644006 8

© *Oxford University Press, 1966*

**Reprinted 1957, 1968, 1969(twice), 1970, 1971, 1974, 1975, 1976(twice), 1978, 1979**

*Made and printed in East Africa*

# PREFACE

This brief introduction to the theory and practice of education is intended for students in the teachers' colleges of Africa. So many English books studied in these colleges lack the necessary emphasis on the African background. Here I have attempted to associate the student's thinking and practice with his own experiences and the lives of his pupils.

It has been difficult to decide the level at which to present the complex ideas associated with the study of education. Many students will not have passed school certificate and all of them will be studying in a foreign language. I have finally decided to aim at the understanding of students of roughly school certificate level for two reasons: first, because the entrance standards to teachers' colleges are steadily rising; secondly, because this book will be used more in the second and third years of training, when a student's general education has progressed well beyond entrance level.

To have over-simplified the English would have required the omission of many topics necessary to proper thinking about education. There is an educational vocabulary which must become familiar to all teachers. In any country the full understanding of this vocabulary will emerge slowly, and only with continued school experience with children. Should it be thought, therefore, that the 'educational jargon' used in this book errs on the side of excess, I suggest that the tutor's imaginative assistance, combined with the student's progress in his general education, will gradually correct this defect. <u>For the first reading perhaps selective study of the more practical chapters will be the best solution.</u>

Here and there repetition of ideas has been deliberate in order to preserve a unity within the topic discussed. In any case, such repetition serves to emphasize the relatedness of all aspects of education.

One final word: learning and teaching are activities. Theory in the head or in the book is useless unless translated into the day-to-day response between teacher, children and their environment. Every subject dealt with in this little book involves a live encounter between people and their immediate surroundings. Hence the suggestions, and they are no more than suggestions, for observation and discussion which appear at the end of each chapter are as important as any theory in the preceding pages. Indeed, in several instances, it would be advisable to do some of the practical exercises before reading the chapter. No good purpose will be served by packing theories into students' minds unless these theories emerge in the end as relevant to real school situations.

The Appendix on 'How to Study' is intended for the students' personal use. It is now over forty years since Graham Wallas reminded those who educate the young that 'teachers are more interested in the results of thought processes than in the processes themselves'. This is still true. It is important that all students should acquire good habits of study, but it is quite essential for those who are forced to learn through the medium of a foreign language. This Appendix is a practical guide designed to achieve that end. Appendix II is a brief glossary of educational terms which may be useful to students for rapid reference; but they should realize that few of the definitions are as adequate as those provided in the body of the book.

There remains the pleasant duty of thanking Miss Joyce Gibbs, Mr H. W. R. Hawes, Professor Eric Lucas and Mr. Tom Nabeta for their helpful criticism and advice. I also thank my wife who resolved the mysteries of the typewriter in order to type my illegible manuscript.

E. B. C.

Makerere,
1964.

# CONTENTS

| Chapter | | Page |
|---|---|---|
| Preface | ... ... ... ... ... ... ... | v |

### Part I: The Foundations

| I | What Education Is ... ... ... ... ... | 1 |
|---|---|---|
| II | The Worlds in which we teach ... ... ... | 7 |
| III | Adapting the Old to the New ... ... ... | 16 |

### Part II: Growing Up

| IV | Nature's Growing Points ... ... ... ... ... | 22 |
|---|---|---|
| V | The Needs of Childhood ... ... ... ... ... | 29 |
| VI | The Needs of Adolescence ... ... ... ... | 39 |
| VII | Individual Differences ... ... ... ... ... | 44 |
| VIII | The Growth of Personality and Character ... ... | 51 |

### Part III: Learning

| IX | Perceiving ... ... ... ... ... ... ... | 57 |
|---|---|---|
| X | Thinking, Concepts and Imagination ... ... ... | 63 |
| XI | Remembering and Forgetting ... ... ... ... | 70 |

### Part IV: Teaching

| XII | The Teacher as a Person ... ... ... ... | 74 |
|---|---|---|
| XIII | Some ways of Teaching ... ... ... ... ... | 81 |
| XIV | Teaching Them to Think ... ... ... ... | 87 |
| XV | Visual and Aural Aids ... ... ... ... ... | 89 |
| XVI | Discipline, Freedom and Responsibility ... ... | 94 |
| XVII | Discipline, Incentives, Punishment ... ... ... | 98 |
| XVIII | The School as a Community ... ... ... ... | 102 |

## Part V: The Organization of Education

| Chapter | | Page |
|---|---|---|
| XIX | The Organization of Schools | 107 |
| XX | The Curriculum | 111 |
| XXI | The Education of Girls and Co-education | 120 |
| XXII | Problems in Planning Education | 125 |

## Part VI: Aims and Ideals

| | | |
|---|---|---|
| XXIII | The Aims of Education for Today | 134 |
| Appendix I | How to Study | 141 |
| Appendix II | Glossary of Educational Terms | 152 |

# PART I

# THE FOUNDATIONS

# I
# WHAT EDUCATION IS

Most books on the principles of education deal first with the aims of education. This book will leave aims to the end, after we have discovered what children are like and in what circumstances they have to be educated. But we can state now what education *is;* and we can state it very briefly: *Education is what happens to us from the day we are born to the day we die.*

Hence, we are all being educated, sometimes well and sometimes badly, whether we are children or parents or teachers. We are being educated all the time, even when we refuse to be taught, even if we do not go to school, even if we think we have finished our education, even when we sleep. We educate ourselves, other people educate us. We learn from the circumstances in which we live, from the things that surround us daily, from the smallest incident that happens to us, whether it be a sharp word from our father or falling off a tree. We just cannot help being educated.

From these observations we may conclude that education deals with persons, society, things and ideas. Using the more usual words in the educational vocabulary, we can extend this statement by saying that education is concerned with individuals, their social environment, their physical environment and their spiritual environment. By environment is meant 'that which surrounds'. Thus, in this instance, the individual is surrounded by, and therefore influenced by, the social, physical and spiritual surroundings in which he lives. All these kinds of education belong together, and each one helps or hinders all the other kinds all the time.

Persons, individual human beings, it will be noted, are at the centre of education. It is with individuals that education begins. As teachers we are chiefly concerned with what an individual person is and how the influences of environment affect him as he grows up; and not only *how* they influence him but *how much*. We have to ask whether certain qualities of a person remain unchanged in any environment, some qualities slightly changed and some wholly changed. We have also to ask how far people can change their environment or control it; whether, for example, we teachers and parents can create surroundings that are good for children, or help to correct the effects of bad environment.

To understand more clearly what education is, it is necessary to deal much more fully with these four elements of education. This will form a large part of what follows in this book. But before going into too much detail let us think a little more about these four elements, viewing them side by side in close relationship. In so doing we shall note how each helps or hinders the others, and also which parts are under our control and which are outside our control. As this book is chiefly concerned with children and teachers we shall bear this fact in mind as we read.

*Individual Persons.* A baby is born with certain physical and mental qualities that are determined at birth. The colour of his skin, of his hair and eyes, the shape of his face and head, are decided by his ancestors, for he inherits these physical characteristics, and environment will not affect them. But whether he is to have good teeth or good eyesight, exactly how tall or strong he is to be, will be partly decided by heredity and partly by environment.

Again, it has been decided at birth how intelligent a person is going to be. We cannot increase his intelligence; all that environment can do—in this case good teaching, good feeding and a good home—is to help him to use his intelligence to the full.

But a human being is not just a body and a brain. He is a *personality;* that is to say he is a being entirely different from all other beings; he is himself and no one else. And this personality grows more distinct from other personalities as he grows up. What kind of personality he becomes will depend very much on the home he is born into, on his parents, brothers and sisters, on the village he lives in, on his school, on the tribe or nation to which he belongs, and on the thousands of things, beliefs and ideas that he will encounter throughout his life. Thus environment, physical, social and spiritual, at least partly, but not entirely, forms his character. But, it must be noted, a human person can also partly change his environment. He can hoe the open bush and turn it into a garden, build a house to shelter him from the weather, reduce the time he has to travel by using a motor car, blow a hole through a mountain or change the course of a river.

In brief, then, a person is a product of his heredity and also of his environment.

*Social environment.* A baby has a mother and a father, and when he is born a family has been created. The family is the first part of his social environment. In Africa, the family may be part of an extended family which belongs to a clan and tribe. His family may live in a village, he may later go to school, to a school in a town, to a teachers' college or to a university. These institutions in Africa today belong to independent African nations. All these units of society, from the smallest (which is the family), to the largest (which is the nation), are part of his social environment.

We cannot choose our parents, and to that extent we cannot control where we are born or the society to which we belong. But every individual is reacting to his social environment all his life. This environment is all the time influencing the way he lives, the occupation he adopts for earning a living, his ideas and beliefs, the way he rears his children. He can accept his community as it is, or he can strive to change it. No one living in Africa today has to go far to see how Africans themselves have greatly changed their own social environment. They have adopted western methods of production in farming and industry and thus transformed their economy; they have created independent nations out of small tribes. It is clear then that part of a man's social environment is under his control. And teachers should note that education plays a most important role in making these changes possible. But whatever happens to him, a man always remains himself, different from all other people, and capable of making his own judgments and choices and directing his own life.

*Physical environment.* The earth is a small planet which revolves on its own axis once in twenty-four hours and revolves round the sun once in a year; hence night and day and the seasons of the year.

It is part of an immense universe consisting of billions and billions of stars and planets whose number man has never counted and whose remoteness defeats the human eye. The universe, and especially the sun, is our physical environment which determines every detail of physical life on earth. Wherever men live on the earth is that part of this environment with which they are most familiar—mountains, plains, deserts, marshes, rivers, trees, plants, rain, drought, soil and rock—these are the more obvious parts of the physical conditions in which men live. But we cannot see all our physical environment, for part of it consists of tremendous physical forces like electricity which are invisible but very real. We know of their presence when we see the results of these forces e.g. in a thunderstorm or when we switch on the electric light. These physical conditions of man's existence largely determine how he lives; but not entirely.

The whole history of man might be described as the story of the way he has conquered his physical environment. He has irrigated deserts and terraced hillsides for his crops, dug deep into the earth for its mineral riches, cultivated hundreds of plants for his food and harnessed electrical power to industrial and domestic use. He cannot entirely control his physical environment; but he can use it by controlling part of it. Even when he weeds his garden he is controlling his environment. The part he controls and the part he cannot control both remain man's physical environment, which affects the lives of all men, and which they can never neglect for a moment. Even schools, we shall see, have a part to play in using their physical environment in the education of children.

*Spiritual environment.* Just as we live in a social and physical world, so we also live in a *spiritual and moral world*. But whereas our social world consists of people and our physical world of natural features and forces, our spiritual environment is made up of *ideas, beliefs and attitudes* whose influence on us is just as powerful as that of the people and things around us. Hence our spiritual and moral environment is of tremendous importance, for *it shapes our minds*, determining how we think and act. More than any other influence it will decide the quality and direction of the teacher's work. For what we believe makes us the sort of men or women we are, and therefore determines how we teach. (See Chapter XXIII.)

All our lives we are being affected by the constant wave of ideas that seem to come to us in the very air we breathe. Every man and woman is like a radio station, receiving all kinds of messages which he has to sort out for himself. Ideas come beating down upon our minds and feelings all day long, and leave their impression for good or ill. Their origins are many and different. They come from our parents and from the traditions our parents have inherited. They come from our religion, from the beliefs we are taught about God and his relationship to men; from our teachers, from the village elders, from impressions made on our minds by books, newspapers and radio, from the market place, from the world of science. And our minds also form their own ideas according to the way we receive impressions from our own experiences: for example, from going to church, or to a political meeting, or an educational conference or to a dance hall.

Many good and bad ideas come into our minds. Men and women today are finding it very difficult to decide which to accept and which to reject. But a choice has to be made if we are to be good men and women. Our choice will depend on the nature of our deepest beliefs and our firmest convictions, for belief and conviction will determine our attitudes towards other people, and in the case of teachers especially, their attitudes towards children. If we believe in God, and that men and women are children of God, that all men are brothers, then our attitude to other people is likely to be friendly and helpful. If we believe that life is a conflict between man and man, our attitude to our neighbour will be filled with hatred and envy.

If our attitudes are friendly, life will be productive and peaceful. If we think of other people as enemies then we shall struggle to get on top, and children in school will be regarded as little enemies and their only use to the teacher a means of earning his wages. If we believe it is essential to be honest at all times, we shall spread the ideas of honesty and truth among our pupils. But if we believe it is a good policy not to tell the truth, or to tell the truth only when it pays, then we shall spread the idea of untruthfulness and add to the amount of dishonesty in our schools and society. Again, if we are too lazy to use the ideas of modern science for the benefit of men and women we shall assist in keeping them poor. Finally, if our ideas and attitudes concerning children are wrong then we shall make bad teachers. There are as many ideas about how to educate children as there are teachers. One of the objects of this book is to sort them out.

### Observations and Practical Work

1. Make a list of the ways in which people earn their living in your **neighbourhood**.

2. Make a chart of your relationships with other members of your family. Compare your results with those of other students in your group. Something like this:

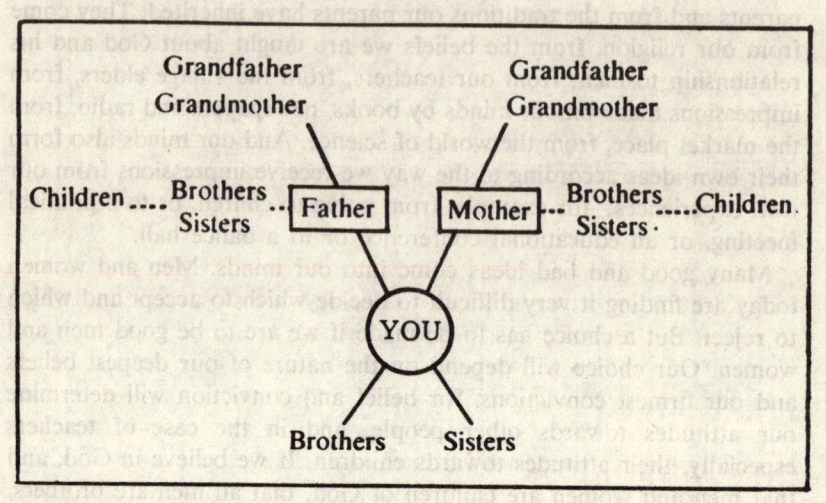

```
        Grandfather              Grandfather
        Grandmother              Grandmother
                    \           /
   Children ---- Brothers  Father -- Mother  Brothers ---- Children
                 Sisters                     Sisters
                              YOU
                         Brothers  Sisters
```

Put in:
a) Time spent with these relations at various ages.
b) Who provides discipline.
c) Who tells stories and passes on traditions.
d) Who gives presents and provides treats.
e) The name by which you know them.
f) The name by which they know you.
g) Who looks after the small children.

(Note: this is an exercise in preparation for the next chapter.)

### Discussion and Essays

1. What is meant by environment? Explain the differences between physical, social and spiritual environment.
2. In what ways do men control their environment? What parts of it are they unable to change?

# II

# THE WORLDS IN WHICH WE TEACH

No man can change the time and place of his birth. Where we were born will to a large extent determine how we live. We are all born into a world which is vast in size, inhabited by millions of people of different races who live in different geographical surroundings. Each of us is born into a particular community in this complex world; and this community is our social environment. We know best the community in which we live from day to day. Teachers work in schools, their pupils come from homes which in Africa usually exist in small villages or towns, all of which are part of a national homeland. For children, life is most real in the home; it is less real in the school, or in the village or town. Young children seldom realize what it means to be a citizen of a country; but they grasp the idea of a national community when they are older.

Hence the work of teachers takes place in the setting of home, school, village, town and nation. These five social groups exist all over the world. But in Africa there also exist the social groups we call tribe and clan, which are of great importance, for from the tribal past come the customs that partly determine how Africans think and behave. All these social groups influence each other. What happens in the home affects the village life; the decisions of national governments reach down to the remotest village or tribe. None of us can now live apart from his neighbours and the rest of the world.

## The Family

The family is the smallest group in society. In the good home a child's needs will be satisfied: his bodily needs of warmth and food, and also his psychological needs of security and love. Unless these four primary needs are satisfied a child cannot develop normally into maturity. In African societies there are broadly speaking two kinds of family. There are the simple, or nucleated, family consisting of mother and father and children only, and the extended family which includes grandparents and the father's brothers and sisters and their children. There may also be polygamous families. The extended family in African societies is very helpful to all its members, for they loyally help each other when in need. This is a feature of African society of which Africans can be proud.

Today this unity of the extended family is breaking down under the pressures of new ways of living. Teachers must be aware of this because these modern changes affect the lives of the children they teach. But the needs of young children remain the same: they must be rightly *fed* and they must feel *secure:* that is, they must feel that they are loved by their parents and that their parents exist to protect and guide them. Where these simple conditions for happy growth are not present, teachers may expect the children of such homes to be difficult to deal with.

*Good Homes.* Good parents will not only supply these basic needs but will also train their children to become good members of their community. They will teach them to help in the home and garden, to be courteous, honest and respectful; they will instruct them in the best traditions of the tribe; they will help them in the use of their native language by story-telling and recitation. Fathers will instruct sons in the affairs of the clan and in the skills of the land; mothers will train daughters in domestic duties and prepare them for motherhood.

Children feel most secure and will grow up with least difficulty when:
a) the relationship between their parents is friendly and helpful,
b) father and mother co-operate in planning family life,
c) both parents are hard-working and sober,
d) both parents set a good example of sensible behaviour,
e) there is enough money and food in the house to feed and clothe the children properly.

The good teacher will try to know not only his pupils but also their parents; because the more he knows of the parents, the more will he come to know of his pupils.

*Bad Homes.* Unfortunately many children in Africa, as in all parts of the world, do not come from good homes. Many parents are very poor and cannot provide sufficient food for their children; many are ignorant and do not provide the right kind of food or clean and healthy conditions in the home; some just do not think education is important and fail to send their children to school; some cannot pay the fees; some are lazy and waste their money on alcoholic drinks and neglect their children badly. These are the worst kind of parents.

But there are also other influences at work which are bad for the home. For example, fathers may be working far from home and hence their children lack the control that the head of a household should give. Mothers spend long hours on land-work and leave their babies untended for the day, or in the care of young children. Still worse conditions exist where homes have been broken by the desertion or divorce of husband or wife. This results in neglect of children at a period when parental care and affection are essential. Researches have shown that children are most neglected in broken homes or in polygamous homes. But it should also be noted that the extended family is more likely to help children whose parents have neglected them, for in this system of mutual help a child becomes the responsibility of the clan.

*All adults are part of the children's social environment.* The most important adults are the parents and other senior members of the extended family. The total influence of the family is stronger than that of the teacher at school. Adult example, both good and bad, plays a most important part in the lives of children. A drunken father will soon find his sons following his example; if the older people of the family are dishonest, dirty, lazy and quarrelsome we must not expect children to avoid these evils easily, unless the school corrects the bad influence of such homes.

*Feeding Children.* Children cannot grow up happily when poverty and ignorance govern family life. If children are not well fed and treated with kindness, they will not be successful in school. *Poor feeding interferes with children's physical and mental growth.* Almost everywhere in Africa infant mortality is high; in some areas one baby in five dies before the age of three years, a terrible wastage of human life. Some African foods, like cassava and banana, lack protein. *Lack of protein* in the diet is especially dangerous, for it may cause the disease called kwashiorkor from which children may die. But in addition, poor diet affects children's learning capacity. Parents and teachers must realize that *hungry children cannot make progress in school*. Well fed children learn more quickly and make more rapid progress, both physically and mentally. It is, indeed, no exaggeration to say that if the undernourished children of Africa enjoyed a simple but balanced diet the resulting educational advance would be quite remarkable.

## The Wider Neighbourhood

The family is the smallest unit in human society. In Africa the bonds which bind people together are the extended family, the clan and the tribe. But today, as we have seen, the nation has become another uniting influence in African life. The independent African nation now unites not only several tribes but even different races.

It is important to note that some of the influences that unite people into one tribe, also tend to separate tribes from each other. Thus tribe, race and language *both bind and separate*. For instance, people who speak the same language and inherit the same customs and loyalties feel themselves to be united in one tribe. But they feel different from and separated from other tribes who speak different languages and have other traditions. The same is even more true when differences of race are added to differences of language and custom. Teachers in schools where there are several tribes, or even races, are well aware of the difficulties of teaching the same subject in two languages at the same time. They would prefer to use one language which all the children can understand.

But on the national scale, tribal divisions present social and political difficulties which touch all Africans. When, for example, we speak of Ghanaians, Nigerians, Tanzanians and Ugandans, we refer to millions of Africans who are politically united within their national frontiers, but have still to solve the problems of tribe and language which separate people in the same country. To break down the barriers of language between people in the same country, statesmen will need the help of teachers. This is one reason why we must realize that the teacher's neighbourhood includes not only home, village and town but also the much wider communities of tribe and nation. It is in this wider neighbourhood that he teaches; this is the wider world in which his pupils will grow up.

## Changing Ways of Living

Ways of living have been changing throughout human history, but the rate of change in the past has been so slow that people were not able to notice any change at all. Today it is quite different. Change in the conditions in which men now live is more rapid than at any other time in the history of men. It is not the mere fact of change but the *rate* of change that is important. We are now living in the most unstable and bewildering conditions that mankind has ever known. We can gather some idea of the rapid rate of change in our lives if we compare the advances made in four of man's activities with which we are all familiar, namely: the means by which he carries his burdens; the ways by which he produces his food; the speed with which he sends his messages; and the means by which he cures diseases.

If we take the last 5,000 years as the period within which we make our time-measurements, then it is clear that there have been greater changes in all these four activities during the last fifty years than in the previous 5,000 years. Goods which fifty years ago were carried by porters are now carried by motor-truck and aeroplane; in agriculture the hoe lifts one pound of earth while the tractor moves a ton; messages that once took months can be sent in minutes by radio; and medical science has replaced magic in curing diseases that once killed millions of men and cattle. Soon man will be able to travel to the moon. Thus the first half of the twentieth century has seen more changes in man's environment than in all the fifty centuries before the year 1900. But wisdom is not the same as knowledge. Though our knowledge is much greater because of all these recent inventions we do not seem to be any wiser than men who lived 2,000 years ago.

All these changes touch the lives of people throughout the world. Not a single man or woman can escape their influence. But in Africa, there are special conditions that result from the last century of Africa's history. One of these is the introduction of the world languages, English and French. These languages are spoken all over the world by at least 400 million people. They are used by Africans as a means of international communication, and in our schools and colleges as a means of higher learning.

There are other changes: for example, the old tribal education has given place to formal schooling; the old mission school is now a part of the state system of education; formal education is no longer confined to the 'Three R's' but extends to secondary and technical schools, to teacher's colleges and universities, which train not only young men but also young women for internationally recognized qualifications.

Perhaps even more important for the future of African nations is the change from subsistence agriculture to the growing of cash crops, i.e. a change from a system where people grew just enough food for their families to systems where they grow crops for sale in the world markets. Another change is that more people work for money wages on farms or in factories and workshops, or on the roads and railways.

Now when people have money to spend, the whole machinery of international trade begins to operate. Africans now buy cloth, pots and pans, bicycles, motor cars and radios from the factories of Britain, Europe, America, India, Japan; and they export their own cotton, coffee, cocoa, palm oil, groundnuts and minerals to pay for what they buy. Again, thousands of African students are attending European and American universities, bringing back with them new knowledge and new ideas. Thus *Africans are now inevitably, and for ever, part of the world of nations;* and independent African states are members of the United Nations where they influence world opinion.

### Two Worlds—the Old and the New

The old ways do not disappear suddenly when the new ways come to take their place. For a long time *the old and the new live together*, side by side. Hence we live, as it were, in *two worlds*. We only have to cast our eyes around our homes to see that this is so—there is the father who cannot read or write and his son of twelve who can; the radio in the hut made of mud and wattle; the little farm tilled by the hoe and the big farm ploughed by a tractor. It is not easy for children to live in two worlds at the same time, in the world of the simple home with old ideas, and in the world of the school where they will learn things of which their parents are ignorant.

Let us consider some of the problems that arouse conflict between the world of the past and the world of the present:

1. *The Tribe* which for centuries has given comfort and security to its members, does not easily fit into the organization of a modern state. The tribe will wish to maintain its ancient rights, but the Central Government may find this an obstacle to national unity. How, then, can we preserve the best in our tribal ways and at the same time fulfil the needs of national government?

2. Consider *agriculture*. Modern agricultural science recommends new methods of farming that will increase the productiveness of the soil. This would enrich the farmer, raise the standard of living and improve the nutrition of children. On the other hand some people think the old ways of farming are best, and are suspicious of what are really better ways, and so they remain poor. How can teachers help here?

3. If we turn to the world of *medical science* again we find two worlds existing side by side. We find hospitals and clinics for healing the sick and preventing diseases, like malaria and bilharzia, from destroying the lives of thousands. African doctors and nurses play a large part in this fight against disease. Unfortunately, we also find that old superstitions about the causes and cure of sickness still hold the minds of many people who prefer ancient magic to modern science.

4. But it is not only on the level of material things that old ways of thinking have to be adapted to new conditions. The views of parents are questioned by their children, for the better educated younger generation are beginning to think for themselves and are unwilling to accept the opinions of their elders. Better education has enabled young people to learn foreign languages which their parents do not understand. In consequence many parents feel shut out from their children's lives. They feel they have lost control over them—like the mother who said, 'I corrected my son in my own language and he answered me in English.'

5. There are other influences that separate children from their parents. In earlier times children spent nearly all their early lives in the home under the discipline of their family and tribe, but now they go to school for most of the day and in boarding schools they are separated from home influences for long periods. They mix with boys and girls from other tribes and are often taught by teachers from other countries. At school they learn new subjects, like science and technical trades, of which their parents are ignorant. They are prepared for work in the national community whose agricultural and industrial needs require instruction which the old tribal education could not give. When trained these young people often seek work far away from their homes and tribal background. All these influences are weakening the bonds of family and tribal life, and many young people are finding themselves cut off from their supporting roots in home and tribe. All these changes, both material and spiritual, are part of the teacher's environment. And he has to realize that he, too, is a product of the same conditions that shape the lives of his pupils.

### The African Environment

One mistake we must guard against. We must not now think of what is called the 'African background' as *old* and the influences of the western world as *new*. We must remember that in Africa this impact of the western world on African ways of life has been going on for over a century, and Africans have to a large extent adapted western ways to their own needs, and made them their own. In this way, much of what we regard as western has now become truly African. History provides scores of examples of one way of life mixing with another in this way. It has happened to every people in Europe and it is still going on. If you are interested in history you will find it a fascinating exercise to discover how often this has happened in the history of peoples during the last 2,000 years.

So when we ask what the environment of Africans is, and what it is to be 'African', the answer is that to be African is to inherit the African past and also to accept Africa as it is *now*. And Africa as it is now, the Africa we have to live in, includes the home and the school, the hoe and the tractor, the medical doctor and the witch-doctor, science and magic, African clothes and European clothes, donkeys and motor cars, men who carry spears and men who carry ball-point pens, women who till the soil and women who teach in school or work in shops and offices, strong tribal loyalties and weakened tribal influences. And at our feet and all around us is the African geographical environment, with its riches still to be exploited and its poverty to be overcome by the intelligent application of man's knowledge and industry. All this wonderful variety is the African world in which African education plays its part. And the good teacher will take note of it all.

This brief description of the African scene suggests that the teacher's task will be both difficult and exciting. It is easy to teach in what is called a *static society* where time stands still, where everything remains the same from generation to generation. All the teacher has to do is to teach what he learned at school in the way he was taught. But when a community is moving on rapidly from one stage of development to another, teachers have to assist in two ways: first, they have to help to preserve the best customs and traditions that give a people its unity, stability and character; secondly, they have to play their part in directing new ideas and practices into the most useful and healthy channels. Briefly, then, schools and colleges have both to *preserve* and to *adapt*.

The children of today are the citizens of tomorrow. Their present happiness and their future usefulness depend on their having *roots* in the community to which they belong; for one of the gravest dangers today is the rootlessness of young people who are hardly conscious of belonging to any community at all. On the other hand, our pupils must learn to adapt themselves to new calls on their intelligence and skill; otherwise people will remain poor and backward, and their children uneducated and hungry.

### Observation and Practical Work

1. Draw a chart to show which members of your family in your grandfather's, your father's and your own generation, a) can read and write, b) know some English, c) have travelled by air.
2. Make a list of the changes that have recently taken place in your neighbourhood, a) in agriculture, b) in transport, c) in education.
3. What three things brought into your area from other countries have changed people's lives most? Give reasons for your selection.
4. Make a list of activities that Africa has happily adopted from western countries, e.g. football.

### Discussion and Essays

1. Define a 'tradition' and give examples from your own country.
2. The importance of the home to the development of young children.
3. 'Adults are part of the children's environment'. Give examples to illustrate this statement.
4. 'To preserve and to adapt.' Discuss what these words mean in relation to old and new ways in Africa.

# III

# ADAPTING THE OLD TO THE NEW

Schools have the important task of preserving traditions that are good for their country. To do this successfully teachers will have to do much thinking. They have to decide not only what old customs are worth preserving but also which of the new influences are to be accepted or rejected. By no means all the new ways of life are good. Some of them are doing harm and should be rejected if African children are to grow up in a healthy-minded society. Here follow a few suggestions of the lines along which teachers' thinking might go.

### The Old Education

Although the tribal education given to our fathers did not include reading and writing, it nevertheless provided types of teaching and discipline that prepared children effectively for the kind of life they were to live. In so far as education is a preparation for life, our forefathers educated their children very well. This principle, that *education is a preparation for life,* is quite the most valuable contribution of the African past to the education of today (see Chapter XXIII). This does not mean that we should use the same practices and methods, but rather that we should have this principle in our minds, and ask ourselves carefully what it implies when we use our modern methods in school. At least teachers should ask themselves whether they are preparing their pupils for the spiritual and practical needs of today by giving them only a diet of reading, writing and arithmetic.

In the old days, education was informal; it was not given in classrooms by trained teachers but took place naturally throughout childhood as children went about their daily occupations. It was given by parents and other members of the extended family. All adults were regarded as teachers of the young, whether it was by example or by insisting on obedience to tribal customs and on good manners. Instruction was given in hunting, cultivation of crops, domestic work and crafts. The children were learning by being useful. Thus, what they learnt was real to them; they knew that it was preparing them to be men and women who could take a useful place in tribal society. They became familiar with the habits of wild and domestic animals, with the uses of trees and plants, flowers and insects. After the evening meal they sang tribal songs, and listened to stories told by their grandparents out of the deep well of tribal folk-lore. These were their 'literature' lessons, from which they also learned correct and vivid speech.

This, then, was an education which gave them roots in their own past, but also gave them the skills which enabled them to live productively in the present. Above all, we must note, their education was deeply concerned with the land, from which they gained their daily food and on which they built their homes. This aspect of African life must never be forgotten, for, as far into the future as we can see, most people in Africa must live on the land.

### The New Education

Today, much of what was once done by parents must now be done by teachers in the changed conditions of modern life. *What then, can modern education do to preserve the good parts of this ancient education?*

In approaching their task teachers should be guided by three simple principles:

*First:* that education should prepare for life;

*Second:* that to apply this principle today it is not necessary to preserve all the old ways and attitudes;

*Third:* that teachers should not just imitate the old ways but should use *the idea behind* them to develop new and better practices suitable for the children of today.

1. The first principle, that schools should prepare children for life, we can accept as self-evident. Its applications are very wide and will form many subjects for student discussion (see Chapter XXIII).

2. The second principle may be illustrated by reference to a specially difficult but very real situation that teachers will have to deal with, namely, how far the older attitudes to people in other tribes should be preserved. More and more children from different tribes and races will be educated in the same class, and more teachers from different tribes and races will teach in the same school. In these circumstances it will not be wise or even possible to use the school to emphasize tribal and racial differences. Again, as more schools are controlled by the public authorities instead of by the various religious bodies, it is most important that religious differences should be accepted in a spirit of friendliness and tolerance, whether in denominational or state schools. The aim of the teacher should be to help all Africans and other races to work and play together and to understand each other. Every tribe and race has much to contribute to the general welfare and happiness of a school. In song and music, for example, children can help each other to appreciate the different contributions of other peoples.

3. The third principle—that it is *the idea behind* the older teaching that matters—will provide the resourceful teacher with the greatest opportunities for applying new ideas. Consider, for example, its application to the age-long contact of children with the land and with the world of nature. Whereas they once learned old-fashioned methods of agriculture they can now be introduced to the more scientific methods. Rural science can be taught by experiments in the school garden so that children can see for themselves that some methods are good and some bad. Thus they will acquire a simple but sound idea of scientific cultivation. The trees, plants and animal life will be studied with more understanding. When they learn how plants grow, how they are fertilized, what conditions are required for healthy growth, their sense of wonder at the marvels of nature will be increased. For modern science not only tells us how to produce crops abundantly, but also reveals more vividly the wonders that lie hidden in the world of nature around the school. Here, then, is one example of using an old idea for modern purposes.

Another example is quite different, and yet closely related. Everywhere in Africa, people are skilled in the arts and crafts. Every school should encourage these ways of self-expression, all of which can be firmly based on African tradition and experience. Unfortunately, owing to lack of money for materials and to shortage of suitable teachers, many children have been deprived of this essential part of their education. But children will not develop into fully educated persons unless they are able to express themselves in these manual and artistic skills, and quite apart from the valuable educational experience we call 'self-expression', the hand and the eye must be trained to deal with far more complicated things than were ever imagined by our forefathers—delicate machinery, woodwork, pottery, and design for all kinds of useful articles that are now coming into daily use.

If the teacher is to be successful in the teaching of the arts and crafts he should observe four principles:

*First:* he should use the resources of the school neighbourhood, the local wood for carpentry, the clay for pottery and modelling, the local reeds, grasses, sedges and other fibres for making baskets and mats, banana bark for picture-making, and so on. By thus using local materials he will not only overcome the difficulty of expense but he will also be training his pupils in the use of their neighbourhood.

*Second:* he should note the traditional patterns employed in making articles for the home, and improve their quality and usefulness where possible.

*Third:* he will help his pupils to make real things and not confine them to dull exercises that are thrown away when made. When children can take home a basket or box or bowl they can see in daily use they will take greater care in making it, and their parents will take a keener interest in the school.

*Fourth:* in teaching drawing, painting and modelling, the teacher should not make children copy his ideas but should leave them free to develop their own. This is of great importance for the development of their imagination and for the expression of their own ideas and feelings. Too often we find a class of pupils in an art lesson who have all drawn the same picture. This means that it is not their own but the teacher's. There is a golden rule for art teaching summed up in the words of a very able African teacher of art: '*Do not copy: copying puts God to sleep.*'

Similar principles apply to *music*. Africans are a music-loving people. That is a dull school which sings no songs and has no orchestra of simple instruments, many of which can be made at school from local materials. Folk-tales can be turned into songs; the simple words of a new language can be learned by singing songs in that language; folk-dancing of African and other peoples will combine with music. Some African musicians are collecting African folk-songs and making song books suitable for schools. Teachers can help in doing the same. So once again the past can feed the present in supplying one of the loveliest and most pleasant parts of education. But, we must remember, music has been made by peoples all over the world since the world began. Most nations are glad to adopt for themselves the songs, tunes and dances of other peoples, and African children will enjoy them just because they are children, for whom singing and dancing are as natural as breathing.

So far we have emphasized the connection between the old and the new patterns of life in African society. But we must be careful not to over-emphasize the old ways for some of them are really out-of-date and will serve no useful purpose. Schools today must face the needs of the future and use new knowledge that has little or no connection with the informal education of our forefathers. All countries have to produce more food and a higher standard of living for all their peoples. This will not be done unless the schools teach science and technical subjects that can be applied to agriculture and industry. We shall say more of this in Chapter XX when we discuss the curriculum.

### Observation and Practical Work

1. On p. 16 we referred to tribal education as a preparation for life. Try and find out from old people what kind of tribal education still exists in your home area. Compare your results with the experience of other students.
2. Discover what children's games, arts, crafts and musical instruments exist (a) in your home area, (b) near the college.
3. Collect local children's songs from home and near the college. Carefully record the words and the tune if you can.

### Discussion and Essays

1. What old customs are worth preserving and why?
2. What can teachers do to break down tribal and racial barriers in their areas?

*PART II*

*GROWING UP*

# IV

## NATURE'S GROWING POINTS

Having discussed the environment in which both children and teachers live we turn to children themselves. This brings us to the essential task of the teacher, which is *to help children to grow up*. If this is the teacher's primary task then it should be evident that the pupil and not the teacher is the most important person in school. Teachers will go wrong from the start of their career if they fail to realize that it is on children that their attention and concern should be focused. It is for this reason that we speak of a 'child-centred' education, that is, a type of education that places children in the forefront of the teacher's mind; not books, or subjects, or the teacher's convenience, but the living, growing, learning child.

One reason for this view of the teacher's relationship to children is the fact that children do a good deal of growing up for themselves, without the aid of either parents or teachers. For nature has given this capacity for growth to every living thing, not least to human beings, whose growth to maturity is more wonderful than that of any other part of the creation. By *growth* is meant growth in size, shape and complexity. To accomplish this growing process nature has provided every child with a set of tools to start them in the first steps of living. This equipment begins to work as soon as a baby is born. Without it he could not take his first breath, utter his first cry or walk his first step. These primary gifts of nature are not acquired by education, but they make education possible. They are *nature's growing points*, that is to say, the starting points from which all other human capacities develop. All of them can be observed in action during the early years of a child's life; all of them remain with us as we pass through life to old age.

## Nature's Growing Points

Here follows a brief summary of the equipment with which every child is born, the natural endowment which enables him to begin the long and complicated process of growing up.

1. *Reflex action.* At birth the almost helpless baby can breathe, cry, blink, sneeze, suck, swallow, digest his food, reject distasteful food. None of these quite complicated acts has been taught, each of them takes place without thought and quite independently of the will. Such action is called *reflex action*. It is nature's first way of preserving life. Without this elementary provision for continuing life, we should all die at birth. We do not have to teach a baby to cry! He does not have to teach himself. He just cries when he feels like it. Reflex action largely controls the first year of life.

But it is obvious that although reflex action will just keep us alive, it will not do much more. So nature provides us with the capacity to make a still more useful kind of reflex which marks the point in human life when we begin to learn. This is the *conditioned reflex*.

2. *Conditioned reflexes.* These new reflexes are *acquired* from our contacts with the conditions around us, i.e. they are 'conditioned' by contact with things, with people, and in the case of the very young child, especially with his mother. Perhaps the first conditioned reflex of a baby is the activity of suckling. His innate power to suck is stimulated by contact with his mother's breast, and he thus learns to find comfort and pleasure when this condition is present. In a more advanced stage, he learns to avoid touching fire or sharp thorns. If he has been frightened by a loud noise or an angry dog, he will seek his mother's protection. Hence, he will be 'conditioned' to avoid painful experiences and to seek pleasureable experience.

These conditioned reflexes are important in education because they help to form habits, both good and bad. They are the basis of home and school training in cleanliness and simple forms of good behaviour. But it should also be noted that conditioned reflexes can have unfortunate effects. When contact with things and people creates fear, fear of the dark or of the hurtful severity of parents or teachers, children may be prevented from growing up in a normal and happy way.

But the main point to note about the conditioned reflex is that a child *learns from the results of his own actions*. This is self-education and the first stage of learning.

3. *The six senses* are another very important part of our natural equipment. First, are the well known 'five gateways of knowledge', the senses of *touch, sight, hearing, taste* and *smell*. But there is also a much less known 'sense' of which we are not conscious because we are quite unaware of what it is doing. This is the sense of 'knowing-where-the-parts-of-our-body-are!' The scientific word for this sense is *kinaesthetic*, from the Greek word which means *to move*. Hence this sense guides movement—of our head, eyes, limbs, fingers and so on. Without this sense we could not stand upright, or walk or write a letter, or put food into our mouths. We would not know where our fingers or toes were. Obviously this sense is important for education—in writing, sewing, all kinds of play, and in fact, every movement we make.

It is through the senses that we are able to experience *pleasure* and *pain*, the two powerful feelings that govern a baby's life, and, indeed, influence a large part of the lives of grown-ups too. We have already noted that the conditioned reflex is based on the feelings of pleasure and pain, which affect the formation of habits. The feeling of pleasure will encourage actions or habits that result in a feeling pleasant to one of our senses; likewise the feeling of pain will tend to prevent actions that cause pain. These facts have obvious lessons for parents and teachers. If for instance, we wish to encourage a child, we should try to give him a feeling of pleasure in the activities we wish him to engage in.

4. *The innate tendencies*. But life cannot be lived satisfactorily on the simple foundation of the six senses or the conditioned reflex. So nature provides us with a more complicated equipment for dealing with the many challenges of life. These are the *instincts* which are inborn in men and animals. Pure instinct in animals can be defined as an inborn drive or need that results in a fixed pattern of behaviour directed to achieve a definite purpose.

In animals instincts nearly always operate according to a fixed pattern. A good example is the periodical urge of a bird to build its nest, and to build it in a certain way. The weaver bird builds nests to one pattern, the eagle in quite a different pattern. The study of the life cycle of the honey bee reveals how totally bees are governed by instinct. The life of the bee has followed the same pattern for millions of years. This is what is meant by our definition of pure instinct. The energy from a particular instinct always flows in one direction, like a river which continuously flows in the same river bed.

But what psychologists once called 'human instincts' are so different from animal instincts that it is better not to call them instincts at all. Today psychologists describe them as *innate tendencies*, or *urges* or *drives*. In human beings these tendencies express themselves in *no fixed pattern* as do the pure instincts of animals. They may be weak or strong in different people, and may be expressed differently on different occasions. For instance, the urge to fight or struggle against an opponent may be expressed in boxing or a game of football or in climbing mountains. Hence it is best not to speak about the 'instincts' of children. We will use the words indicated above to explain children's behaviour.

These innate urges, which prompt children to act in certain ways in certain circumstances, are familiar to any observant parent or teacher. We shall study these patterns of behaviour in more detail in the next chapter. Here we should note certain of their characteristics which are important for teachers:

(a) They are *innate*, i.e. inborn, part of nature's provision to help children to grow up.
(b) They exist in all children but they appear in different degrees of intensity in different children.
(c) Because they are weaker than the pure instincts of animals, they *can be controlled more easily* and directed to the fullest development of a child's personality. This fact is of great importance for it explains why children can be educated.

But the strong feelings or *emotions* created by the innate tendencies of human beings could not be controlled either by teachers or by the children themselves unless nature had made provision for controlling them.

Once again, nature supplies the need. She has endowed human beings with *intelligence*.

5. *Intelligence.* This is the last of nature's growing points. By giving him intelligence nature enables man to manage his own affairs.

We have not each been endowed with an equal share of intelligence; but we have all inherited a share, and the way we use it will decide how we make use of nature's other gifts in the process of growing up.

Intelligence enables us to acquire knowledge, to use it wisely and to apply it usefully. Without intelligence, we should be able *to feel* but not *to know*. It is important to note the difference between intelligence and knowledge because they are often confused. Intelligence is a gift we are born with; knowledge is what we learn. By acquiring knowledge we do not become more intelligent; but the knowledge we acquire assists us to use our intelligence more effectively.

### Growing Points Beyond Nature

We noted above that intelligence enables us to exercise *some* control but not *complete* control over our innate tendencies. Hence intelligence does not solve all life's problems by giving us a ready-made machine for controlling our lives. Nature seems to say 'I will give you the tools; but you must finish the job.'

We cannot proceed with the job of growing up only by the application of intelligence to our behaviour. Intelligence may tell us *how* to behave but it will not necessarily make us *want* to behave in the best way. It may guide us where to go or indicate what we ought to do, but it will not provide *the urge that leads to action*. This is true of all adults but is especially true of children, because their desires are not yet under control. They need a sense of direction. What gives a sense of direction is an aim to be attained by our own efforts, a goal to aim at. If, for example, a boy wishes to excel at football, he should be willing to accept the discipline necessary for acquiring the bodily skills that make this possible. He will practise kicking the ball; he will submit himself to training from a skilled footballer. Thus he combines his intelligence and his desires to achieve his goal. His intelligence and innate urges work together in unity. He controls other desires that may prevent the achievement of his purpose.

Thus it is *purpose* that directs the use of our intelligence and of all the other capacities with which we are endowed. The man without purpose is a lost man; he never knows what he ought to be doing, even if he has lots of intelligence; although without the use of his intelligence he will be equally lost and unable to achieve his aims. So, *we have to add to nature's equipment what nature has not provided*. This is the task of education. It is chiefly parents and teachers who help young people to acquire aims in life so that their intelligence is properly used.

Our argument has now taken us from the reflex and conditioned reflex, through the senses and innate tendencies to intelligence and on into the world of purpose. We shall see this 'purpose-full' striving even in the youngest children, when, for instance, they try to touch their toes or to reach a pretty ball or flower. This purposeful striving is the very beginning of the more advanced and complicated striving of older children and adults. In older children purpose may be expressed in their desire to learn school subjects or to excel in games. In adults purpose may take the form of the pursuit of an ideal, for example, the ideal of the good parent, or good teacher, or doctor or farmer or social reformer. Sometimes, purposeful striving will be concentrated on a more self-centred ambition, like that directed by the desire to become a rich man. But whatever the purpose, its effect is to bring all parts of the human personality into concentrated action.

Teachers cannot do much about the reflexes. But they can do a great deal to help children to use fruitfully their emotional energy. And they can assist children to use their intelligence to the fullest extent and in the most useful ways. Teachers can also help children to form healthy ideals. In these ways a teacher helps children to grow up, which is the primary duty of those who educate.

One further point must be emphasized. Neither children nor teachers live in a vacuum. We have already seen that we all live in a vivid, interesting and complicated environment, physical, social and spiritual. It is impossible to live as isolated beings uninfluenced by the people among whom we live. Our innate tendencies and intelligence are responding to the stimulus of our social environment every hour of the day. There is a continuous two-way traffic between persons and their surroundings, a continuous *process of adaptation and response*. Children adapt themselves to life at home by responding to the wishes of their parents and to the needs of other members of the family. They adapt themselves to the demands of school life, and respond to the stimulus of teaching and school experience. It is part of the teacher's task to help children to respond to the circumstances in which they live so that they eventually grow up into unworried, useful and stable persons.

### Observation and Practical Work

1. During your vacation or in the demonstration school, observe five children for a week and make notes on:
    (a) activities that seem to be constructive,
    (b) activities that have been learned e.g. writing,
    (c) activities that show purposeful striving.

2. Observe a pupil or a fellow student for half an hour and make a list of his actions that can be placed under one or other of the following headings:
   (a) conditioned reflex,
   (b) sense stimulus,
   (c) intelligence.
3. Give examples of adaptation and response:
   (a) in village life,
   (b) in school life.

**Discussion and Essays**

1. The differences between the instincts of animals and the instinctive tendencies of children.
2. The influence of purpose in deciding how we use our intelligence.

# V

## THE NEEDS OF CHILDHOOD*

In the previous chapter we learnt that the innate tendencies were a source of emotional energy and that our intelligence and a sense of purpose help us to control this energy. We also noted that the people among whom children live will largely determine how they grow up. In this chapter we shall examine in more detail what these innate tendencies are and how they appear in children. For we must realize that the behaviour of children is more frequently decided by their innate urges than by the conscious use of their intelligence. At the same time we should realize that intelligence, too, steadily plays its part as children grow older.

Any observant teacher will see these tendencies at work in the behaviour of his pupils both in and out of school. He should take careful note of them because he will never become expert in the management of children unless he understands the causes that underlie the many types of behaviour he sees among children in their work and play.

One particular point must be emphasized here. In every type of behaviour we are about to study, a child is really expressing a *need*. The good teacher will discover what this need is and supply it, or help

---

*Before reading this chapter make a list of the things children enjoy doing. Then see how many of them are mentioned here.

the child to supply it for himself. All the time, and quite unconsciously, children are striving towards their next stage of growth. They are incomplete persons—ignorant, insecure, small and weak, dependent. They desire to know, to feel secure, to be big and strong, and to be independent. They strive to become complete persons (see Chapter VIII). This is the natural urge that makes growth possible. Teachers who understand what is happening to children as they grow up will be able to assist in the process.

The following is a summary of the most important characteristics of childhood. There is little described in the following pages that an observant teacher will not see in the classroom and playground.

*Anger*. Children show angry feelings when they are prevented from doing what they want to do. When this happens we say they are *frustrated*. A baby will be angry because he is hungry and needs food; he will be angry if deprived of a toy; he will be angry if you hold his legs so that he cannot kick or crawl. Frustration, and therefore angry feelings, occur in children when they find a task too difficult. They hate to feel defeated but cannot find a way to success. These are elementary examples of a child expressing a need through anger, in this case the need for food, for play, for physical movement and for success in a task.

But there is also a less obvious need illustrated by these simple examples. This is the need for a child to learn how to discover for himself the things he is able to do and those he cannot do. Thus anger is a quite normal reaction in the earliest years, but as a child grows older, he will gradually learn that anger does not take him far. With wise guidance and suitable explanation he will learn to understand and control his frustrations. Control of anger is a great step towards maturity. It is important for teachers to understand the meaning of 'frustration' if they are to understand children.

*Fear*. All animals and human beings experience the emotion of fear. This is one of nature's means of assisting us to avoid danger. This tendency is partly inborn and partly acquired by experience or *imitation*. For example, we may have seen a bush buck and its calf suddenly appear by the wayside. The calf is not frightened and does not run away until it sees its mother dash for cover. Here the calf is afraid because its mother is afraid. Similarly many fears of children are the result of parental warning or example. African children are quite unafraid of domestic animals; quite small children happily herd their father's cows because they know there is nothing to fear. But if parents are afraid of thunder or of the dark or of dogs, their children will be afraid too.

Thus we can say that children experience fear and that it is useful to be afraid of dangerous things. But it is also true that fear is an emotion that may have a disturbing effect on a child's development. This is because fear prevents the expression of other tendencies necessary to healthy growth. For instance, children need to feel secure, and fear destroys their sense of security. Fear of a harsh father will prevent a child from behaving freely and sensibly. Fear of a severe teacher may dam back a child's flow of energy and retard his progress at school. Hence education through fear is bound to be a bad form of education.

*Self-will or self-assertion*. This is an important characteristic of childhood for from it may develop valuable human qualities. At about the age of two a child tries to control his little world, especially his mother. He wants everyone to submit to his will. The second year is probably the angriest time of a child's life, because he finds that the people and things around him are not going to be subdued. He begins to exercise his will; he angrily objects to interference and strives hourly to assert himself and have his own way. His parents say 'he has a will of his own', and parents who do not understand children may wish to 'break his will'. This they may easily do by threats and punishment But to break a child's will is to damage a large part of his personality, for self-will is the foundation of self-confidence which in turn develops strength of character.

If a child is threatened and subdued in his early years, if all his natural impulses to push and pull and crawl into forbidden places are thwarted, he is likely to become a sullen fearful child. He may be quiet, 'good', but only half alive. For he will have lost the will and vitality to explore his little world for himself, which nature intended him to do. He will not learn to overcome obstacles; his early self-confidence will be over-shadowed by feelings of insecurity and anxiety.

How then do we use these awkward but essential self-assertive impulses of a child without creating disorder in the home or classroom? One excellent answer given by a well-known psychologist is: 'If a child wants to do anything naughty, teach him how to do it.' If he wants to climb a tree show him how to climb safely; if he wants to dig the garden give him a little hoe and show him how to dig. Briefly, give him plenty to do and show him how to do it. It is much easier to control and teach a busy child than an angry or listless child. In this way self-will is transformed into the will that builds up character —indeed will *is* character, or rather character *in action*. Destructive impulses are directed into constructive ways, and children really begin to control their little corner of a rather perplexing world.

A child will also learn that some things he is not able to do because he is not skilful or strong enough, and some things he must not do because they are dangerous. But when he is allowed to do *the things he wants to do and can do*, he will accept more easily the teacher's refusal to allow him to do the forbidden things.

Sometimes this impulse of self-assertion is expressed in another way. A child may become very proud of some new achievement and want us to take notice of it. He is delighted by his success—'Look how high I can jump! Aren't I clever?' This is quite natural. He is feeling his little *self*, and young children are very *self-centred*. A quiet word of encouragement is all he needs; there is no necessity to tell him he is conceited for he is merely taking another step in growing up.

*Self-submission.* This tendency is clearly the opposite of self-assertion. It should not be confused with fear. It is the desire to escape from people and avoid attention. We shall meet this submissive child in the infant classroom. He runs away from the crowd and does not play with other children. Possibly he is seeking for affection which he cannot find in the rough and tumble with other children. Kindly interest by the teacher and a quiet show of affection will help to establish his self-confidence.

Sometimes we see a strange combination of submission and aggressiveness. A child may assume an aggressive attitude to other children when he has no confidence in himself, perhaps due to failure in his lessons or to ridicule of older children at home. This is an attempt to prove to himself that he is really self-confident and as clever as his class-mates. He tries to acquire confidence by *appearing* to be confident and superior. The remedy in this case is to help him to do one or two things well. Make him responsible for, say, collecting the books, cleaning the blackboard; help him a little with his school work. When he has got one sum right he will feel a little better. When he ceases to be worried about himself he will not worry other children.

*Imitation.* From the earliest years children tend to imitate their parents and later their teachers and fellow pupils at school. A baby imitates the sounds made by his mother and thus takes his first steps in speech. He may imitate the way his parents eat or walk or their way of talking. Any peculiarity of a teacher is most likely to be imitated. Some children imitate more than others. Imitation is quite unconscious in the early years but more consciously used after the age of six or seven. Clearly this capacity to imitate has important results in school. A child will learn by imitating a person performing a skilled task A child will imitate bad behaviour as well as good. He will imitate the bad behaviour of parents and schoolmates just as easily as good behaviour.

There are two interesting developments of a child's tendency to imitate which have important consequences for education.

(a) In purely imitative behaviour, a child merely takes over the *actions* of others. But he will often also take to himself the feelings of those in close contact with him (parents and teachers); and later on he may unconsciously *accept the ideas* of those for whom he has respect. This is because all children in varying degrees are *suggestible*, some much more so than others. The *suggestibility* of children is important in education because a child may be persuaded to perform a task by *suggestion* when he would disobey a direct command.

(b) The second extension of imitation is what psychologists call *identification*. To imitate is to *act* like others; to be suggestible is to *feel* like others; but sometimes a child either imagines he really *is* another person, or at least desires to become exactly like the admired person—i.e. he identifies himself with the admired person, a hero of some kind, father, teacher, footballer, explorer, hunter and so on. It is obviously important that this chosen model with whom the child identifies himself should be a person worthy of imitation. Identification is not general among young children, but during adolescence it may have an important influence in the formation of ideals.

*Curiosity.* Children are naturally inclined to explore and discover the world around them. Their curiosity never seems to be satisfied. They begin by examining the objects close at hand and noticing the differences between them. This ability to distinguish between different things and people is an essential step in learning. Curiosity also prompts children to ask questions. Such questions should be answered, and if not directly answered, the child should be shown how to get the answers for himself. If he is constantly forbidden to touch and explore and inquire, he may lose interest in life and come to regard adults as obstacles instead of helps to his exploration of the world. Teachers should encourage this inborn urge to explore, and schools should make ample provision for stimulating children's curiosity. Classrooms should have a plentiful supply of materials and objects which encourage children's inquiries, for their desire to know is a valuable instrument ready for the teacher's use.

*Collecting.* Many children experience great satisfaction in collecting all kinds of objects which attract their attention—coloured stones, beads, seeds of plants and trees, pieces of string and wire, shells, curiously shaped bits of wood, insects, the bones of small animals, and so on. This interest may absorb their attention feverishly for a time, and then stop.

Obviously the collecting activity can be very useful in helping children to learn. By suitable encouragement, children can be taught to make collections of grasses, plants, insects, stones, pictures, which will make a fine display in the classroom and enormously increase the children's knowledge of the world of nature around the school. Thus the classroom can become a living museum gradually built up by the children themselves. Valuable learning and teaching material is provided and the activity of learning becomes a joint activity in which both teacher and children take part.

*Construction.* Nothing is more obvious to the observer of children than their love for making things. Set a young child before a pile of sand or mud, give him a few blocks of wood, and he will soon be handling them and building shapes out of them. First he will move slowly and experimentally to discover what his material will do. Later on he will begin to build more purposefully, constructing his idea of a familiar object like a house or shelter or bicycle. His skill in these constructive activities will increase steadily.

No teacher should neglect this constructive drive in children for it is the foundation of several aspects of learning, e.g. early ideas of number, the use of materials, the feeling for thickness, weight, length and breadth, judgment of space and shape. A child is also acquiring manual skill by using the small muscles of the hand which develop slowly. At the same time he is satisfying deep emotional urges which if unexpressed in creative activity may well burst forth in destructive ways. Thus he becomes more skilful and at the same time better behaved, because his whole personality is fully engaged on a self-imposed task.

Unfortunately, many African children are not always able to enjoy these opportunities. There are two reasons for this. In the first place, too many African parents think there is no need for these childish occupations. Even in the rural areas, where there is material for making toys, parents often insist that their children sit quietly apart and 'be good', which really means 'do nothing'. Many parents prefer a tidy home to a happy child. In the second place, many children live in homes where there are no toys or materials that can easily be used in this way. This is especially true of children who live in poor homes in towns. Primary schools are often so badly equipped and some teachers too indifferent to provide local materials, that the children get little opportunity for developing their constructive abilities. This lack of manual skill is a great disadvantage in later years.

In more fortunate homes and schools where simple toys and apparatus are provided, it is found that children acquire more manual skill than children in poor homes and schools. Schools must therefore make every effort to supply this need. There is no necessity for expensive toys; the chief need is to encourage this constructive urge by providing as many simple local materials as possible. Teachers, too, should engage in these constructive activities, demonstrating to their pupils that skilled manual work is a highly respectable occupation for any person, no matter how learned he may be. One of the finest carpenters the author has known was a university professor of mathematics!

*Play.* Here we refer to the spontaneous play of children, not to organized games—to the kicking and crawling of infants, to the romping, pushing and pulling, running and jumping, hide and seek, singing and shouting, make-believe games like imitative fighting with spears, that children delight in. This type of play is primarily activity for its own sake. But it is rather more than this. It is activity and pleasure combined; and although the play of children seems to be no more than the expression of happy spirits, it also has a biological purpose. Like the play of puppies and other young animals, it is a preparation for the more serious occupations of later life. In other words it is unconscious *self*-development. Children do not play in order to become strong or skilful in using their arms and legs; nevertheless by playing, without any other impulse than the desire to play, their bodies become stronger and their limbs more skilful.

Another important aspect of the play impulse is the way in which it gathers together several of the other inborn tendencies we have discussed above. Imitation, curiosity, self-assertion, and especially the constructive tendency, can all be seen in children's play. Thus, quite naturally, *play brings together many of the essential growing points of a child's development.* For this reason it is of immense importance in education.

Here are some of the values of play both physical and emotional that should be noted by teachers:

1. Physical play exercises the larger muscles, stimulates the respiratory system and blood circulation, aids digestion and increases control of the finer muscles in the performance of delicate hand movements, e.g. writing and drawing.
2. Play of all kinds provides relaxation from dull and difficult tasks enabling children to refresh themselves and prepare for further work.
3. Free play with playmates helps children to adapt themselves to other children easily and naturally. They learn to co-operate, to share, to lead and to be led, to defend themselves and to defend others.
4. Play helps children to discover themselves. For example a child who is weak at lessons may acquire self-respect in being successful in games.
5. In play a child's whole energies are engaged. Therefore it is most helpful to introduce elements of play into the classroom, especially in the infant school where so much can be learnt by the 'play way'. This often involves the need for children to work in groups where learning and play go happily side by side. It has been found that children learn most rapidly when their tendencies and interests are all engaged when they are learning. Play provides these conditions.

The spirit of play, of course, is not confined to young children. It is one of the happier of human characteristics that develops into new forms as we grow older. When the play spirit dies in a man, an essential part of his human nature dies too. Readers of this book may like to work out for themselves how the play-spirit develops into the varied activities of older children as they pass through primary to secondary school and on into the world. Teachers especially should ask themselves whether they have forgotten how to play. If they have forgotten, then they are not likely to be very good teachers.

Two further comments must be made before we close this chapter. First, it must not be thought that all these innate tendencies will be observed in all children all the time, or that they will appear in every child with the same intensity. All we can say is that most of them will be observable at one time or other in most children of primary school age. Some of them will remain for much longer periods, perhaps for life. As a rule, when an innate tendency has played its part in helping a child to pass on to its next stage of growth, it will weaken and seem to disappear. Anger, fear, self-assertion and submission, for example, may become less necessary to a child's development and quietly give way to other needs. But they may appear again in some form if the child feels frustrated. There is something wrong, for instance, with a child who has ungovernable fits of temper at the age of five, for this type of anger normally reaches its peak at two years. In such a case, we should try to discover the cause of frustration.

The other comment that must be made is this: Although many parents do not object to children's play in the first four or five years, they tend to frown on any activities that are not obviously going to be useful in later life. This attitude is quite understandable, for life in Africa is often hard and the need for producing food exceeds all other needs. Unfortunately, this attitude is even stronger when the children go to school, for here, parents believe, children should sit glued to their desks and learn their lessons. Play is not work; therefore, they say, school should be only for learning useful subjects that will earn wages later on. They frown on the artistic activities, for example, that are a form of play. But creative play as we have described it is an essential activity that enables children to learn the useful subjects more quickly and more effectively. Teachers, therefore, who believe in modern education founded on the nature of children, will use all the growing points nature has provided for helping children to grow up and to learn as they grow.

## Nursery Schools

This is a suitable place to say a word about nursery schools. Some parents want nursery schools to be established so that their children can learn to read and write before they go to primary school. This is quite wrong. Children of pre-primary age are not ready to learn to read and write. (see p. 50). Nursery schools can be excellent schools for little children if they are used in the right way. Their chief purpose is to give children the opportunity to learn to play together, to share toys, to use their hands and feet and eyes, to gain self-confidence, to learn how to keep clean, how to dress, how to use their bodies. A good nursery school will provide all the simple materials and toys and tools which cannot be provided at home. The children will also sing and recite poems which will improve their speech. These are the purposes of a nursery school. Later on, the primary school will soon teach the children to read and write and introduce them to the mysteries of number.

### Observation and Practical Work

1. On teaching practice select *two* children in the class you teach most frequently and try to discover:
   (a) on what occasions they become frustrated,
   (b) on what occasions they concentrate on a task you have set them.
2. Make a list of the games you played at home between the ages of 5 and 10. Do the same with the children in one class you teach. Did your parents encourage you to play games?
3. Choose one child in a class and note the number of times during one day he imitates you or any of his fellow pupils.
4. Try to discover during one morning session in one class how far children were unconsciously working and playing *at the same time*.

### Discussion and Essays

1. What is 'frustration'? What are its causes?
2. How can the 'collecting' and 'constructive' interests of children be used to help children's learning?
3. The importance of play.
4. How does 'play' assist 'work'?

## VI

## THE NEEDS OF ADOLESCENCE

In most African societies there is a ceremony to mark the passage from childhood to adolescence. The rites associated with this ceremony usually include circumcision and other practices designed to impress the young person with the important changes taking place in his physical and social life. Childhood is over; but adulthood is not yet attained. The period in between is called adolescence, a Latin word which simply means 'growing up'. It is a most important period of development, just as important as infancy in deciding the kind of person the adolescent is to become.

There is no sudden break between childhood and adolescence. The development is gradual but definite. Childhood ends at 10 or 11, adolescence begins at 12 or 13 and continues on to 18 or 20 years. There is no fixed age for these stages of growth; individuals differ greatly and boys are usually slower in development than girls. The problems of infancy seem to be repeated in adolescence. The need for self-control of the body and of the emotions still exists. The self-centred infant still lives on in the sensitive 'self-regarding' youth. These young people of 15 or 16 may seem to be physically strong and self-assured; but parents and teachers have to realize that their needs are as real as those of children in the infant school. They may be big, but they are not mature.

*Physical changes.* During adolescence the bones and muscles grow rapidly in strength and weight. Between 11 and 16 a well-fed boy's weight doubles; by 16 a girl has attained her full height. The special characteristics of the male and female develop rapidly. Boys become more masculine, girls more feminine as nature prepares them for their roles as fathers and mothers. The rapid growth of bone and muscle demands good food, especially protein, and plenty of vigorous exercise. Adolescents greatly enjoy team games and dances, and strive to acquire increased skill in them. Boys in particular like to display their strength and skill in physical performance.

*Intellectual and emotional development.* Intelligence develops smoothly throughout childhood and adolescence. But the peak of mental development is reached at the age of 16 although small development after this age may continue in some adolescents.

Most important at this period is the development of *special aptitudes,* i.e. abilities which, while partly dependent on general intelligence seem to be present in some people and not in others. Such aptitudes may be verbal, mathematical, musical, artistic, mechanical or spatial, (i.e. a sense of form and space such as is needed in an architect.) We shall deal more fully with special aptitudes in the next chapter. Here we note that although they appear in childhood they become more evident in adolescence. But these special aptitudes may wither away if they are not used at school. That is one reason why the curriculum of a secondary school should include studies that encourage these special abilities.

Adolescent boys and girls are very sensitive to the approval and disapproval of the people they live with. In their mental and emotional life they think more critically and feel more deeply. Because they desire the approval of other people they exercise greater control over such childish emotions as anger and fear. Anger is much more likely to be expressed in words rather than blows. Adolescents take more interest in the social affairs of school, in clubs and societies and later on in the affairs of the nation.

The adolescent is still highly conscious of himself and sensitive to adult criticism. He desires more responsibility for he is confident that he can manage his own affairs. But adolescents are often treated like children although expected to behave like adults. With some reason they resent adult interference, but there are moments when these perplexed young people crave for support and understanding. And underlying all their problems of dependence and independence, the struggle to be free in a world ruled by interfering adults, there are the disturbing and exciting urges of sexual growth which arouse interest in the opposite sex.

Thus an adolescent lives in *two worlds* at the same time. He craves for independence but often feels dependent. He resents parental correction but needs his parents' sympathy and help. He thinks he knows much and suddenly finds he does not know enough to solve his problems. He wishes to control his own life but finds life full of frustrating obstacles. Hence he may be aggressive or rebellious one day, and co-operative and affectionate the next.

These characteristics of adolescents apply in different degrees to young people in many parts of the world. But it is important to realize that growing up takes on different patterns according to what the community expects of young people. If it is the ideal of parents that men should be aggressive and masterful and women submissive to men, then their aim will be to produce these types in boys and girls. If men and women are regarded as equals then boys will be taught to respect girls.

In an earlier chapter we spoke of the 'two worlds' of the African past and the African present. In a similar way adolescents live in 'two worlds', the world of childhood and the world of adulthood. Young Africans are indeed faced with more difficulties than many young people. They have their own personal problems to solve, they have to adjust themselves to their parents and teachers who seem to curb their desire for independence; and they have to sort out the two worlds of the tribal Africa into which they are born and the new Africa in which they have to earn their living. At a time when ideals are formed their loyalties are pulled in different directions—to their own personal ambitions, to their friends, to their families and tribe, and to their nation. It is the job of parents and teachers to help them to discover for themselves how to behave, how to control their feelings, how to form their ideals, how to become good and useful men and women.

There is no perfect set of rules for the proper treatment of adolescents. Teachers in training should remember that they themselves have only just passed through this phase and should turn their minds back to their recent past and examine their own adolescence. Here we suggest a few principles to help your thinking.

1. Provide ample outlet for physical adventure, leadership and the exercise of initiative, the development of skill in games and the satisfying of constructive and artistic abilities.

2. Give boys and girls *real* things to do—useful things to make for the school such as a cycle shed, the chapel altar cloth, a job in the library, organization of school clubs and societies.

3. Encourage rather than ridicule and condemn. Ridicule is a poison when used by parents and teachers. It dries up youthful ambition and striving.

4. Spread responsibility as widely as possible. A sense of responsibility is a wonderful maker of stable character. It establishes self-respect by enabling young people to believe that they are trusted. Do not wait until you think a boy is responsible; make him responsible by giving him a job to do.

5. Adolescents should be encouraged to think hard and to work hard. Now is the time for stretching their mental capacity, for learning how much there is to know. Allow them to hold no opinion unless they have good reasons for holding it.

6. Develop relationships of friendliness and co-operation with adolescents rather than attitudes of authority and domination. Treat them as equals whenever possible. You will help them to grow up by removing their suspicion that you think they are still children.

7. Use the group loyalties and growing social sense of adolescents in forms of self-government—school council, school clubs and societies run by the boys and girls themselves. Guide their interest in politics by insisting on *informed* discussion.

8. See that they not only talk about ideals but put them into practice. Religion is *doing* as well as *believing*. Too much day-dreaming is not good for young people. They must learn to live on the ground, not in the clouds. But they are interested in *applied* religion. African youth will be better employed in helping the unfortunate e.g. by taking literacy classes in the villages, than in uninformed political discussion

### Maturity

Infancy, childhood and adolescence are stages on the way to maturity. What is a mature person? This is a complicated question which we shall try to answer simply. A mature person has at least the following qualities:

(a) He is able to accept himself as he is, knowing his abilities and weaknesses for what they are.

(b) He believes in himself and confidently pursues his ideals.

(c) He has a sense of humour—which means that he can laugh at

himself more easily than at others, and that he is not hurt when others laugh at him.
(d) He fearlessly accepts responsibility because he believes in himself and the power he possesses.
(e) He is free from self-pity and can accept criticism constructively.
(f) He is not dismayed by failure nor overcome by success.
(g) He can preserve self-esteem with humility, and dignity without self-display.

When we look into ourselves or observe the actions of other adults we are bound to conclude that some of us are not fully grown up. We often see the signs of childhood and adolescence in ourselves and in others. We need not worry, for the process of growing up takes a life time. Faults at twenty can be corrected by the age of thirty, but only if we are conscious of them. If we get angry at disappointment we are childish; if we resent criticism we are adolescent still. If we refuse responsibility we lack the confidence of maturity. If we boast of our exploits we are like the normal child of ten; and if we cannot laugh at ourselves we are lost. A good teacher may not like the class to laugh *at* him, but he should enjoy a good laugh *with* the class, even at his own expense. Nothing is more important for children than that they should grow up among people who are really grown up, people they desire to 'grow up to'. So a teacher has to be a mature person if he is to do his job well. With God's help he has to learn to *make himself*.

### Observation and Practical Work

1. Write down what you think are (a) your best qualities, (b) your weaknesses. Discuss the results with a good friend.
2. Which period at school did you enjoy most? Do you know why?
3. Work out a scheme in which responsibility can be given to many people in school.

### Discussion and Essays

1. How can secondary school students have
   (a) opportunities for physical adventure,
   (b) outlet for applied religion, i.e. social service?
2. What is meant by 'informed discussion'?

# VII

## INDIVIDUAL DIFFERENCES

The education of children would take a great step forward if, on facing his class each Monday morning, every teacher would quietly say to himself, 'God made each one of these children different from all the others; every one is a unique person who needs my help'.

Children differ from each other physically, in temperament, in their inborn intelligence and in their special aptitudes. We shall discuss these differences in turn.

### Physical Differences

Physical differences between children of similar ages stand out clearly when we observe them in class or at play. Some are tall, some are short, or plump or thin, clumsy or agile, strong or frail. Facial expression, the shape of head, nose, chin, the set of their eyes, all add to these variations in physical appearance. Such physical characteristics are inherited. As we have seen, growth in adolescence may modify some of these features. The slightly built boy of ten becomes the tall young man of fine physique; the plump little girl a graceful young woman. But the basic physical characteristics remain throughout life.

### Temperamental Differences

Much more subtle and less recognizable are the temperamental differences in children. These we shall discover only by intimate contact with individuals at work and play.

Temperament may be defined as the expression of those mental and emotional qualities that do not depend on intelligence. We cannot discover a person's temperamental qualities until we see him behave. His behaviour will be largely determined by his temperament as it reacts to the desires he feels within himself and to the demands other people make upon him. This behaviour will take the form of physical, emotional or mental activity which will give the observer a rough idea of his temperament.

When next you find yourself responsible for a class of ten-year-olds, pay special attention to their faces and to their behaviour in and out of the classroom, for, say, a whole week. Or, if you wish to concentrate on a smaller number, choose ten children and study them for a longer period. You will not discover a great deal in this time, but you will find enough to convince you of their temperamental differences. There will be children who are lively, noisy, self-assertive, over-confident, co-operative, sociable children; others may be rather solemn, shy, submissive, quiet, timid. Closer acquaintance would reveal many other differences among them. You would discover amazing powers of perseverance in some, lack of staying power in others; children who attracted friends, a few who were lonely; others excitable or calm, patient or impatient, impulsive or cautious, steady and reliable, or unstable and unreliable. Combinations of these and other qualities form an individual's temperament.

Temperament seems to be a product of both heredity and environment. In so far as it is innate it is dependent on what physiologists call the ductless glands—the thyroid, adrenal, pituitary and sex glands —which pass fluids into the blood stream. Chemical substances in these fluids, called *hormones,* affect bodily growth and temperament. The way in which hormones affect temperament is not known, but it is now generally believed that they are the physiological foundation of the temperamental differences between individuals.

But temperament is also a *product of social experience.* If we irritate a naturally short-tempered child we may make him more irritable; if we laugh at a naturally shy and sensitive child we may increase his tendency to shyness. Similarly, the timid child may lose his timidity by encouragement; the unsociable child may gradually feel more confidence among other children. The lesson to be learnt here is that the behaviour of children is only partly due to inborn qualities of temperament. It is remarkable how children will learn to control their behaviour as they grow up and become quite stable characters.

Temperament cannot be accurately measured, but sensitive and observant teachers can learn to judge children's temperaments well enough for practical purposes. Unfortunately, teachers tend to be more interested in the physical and mental performances of children because these can be measured on the playing field and in examinations. But teachers should pay just as much attention to the temperaments of children, because a child's school progress depends greatly on the temperamental qualities that determine how effectively intelligence is used. This accounts for the fact that some brainy children fail in school and in later life, whereas less clever children may succeed. The difference between them is a difference of temperament, not of ability.

### Differences in Intelligence

Intelligence is rather like electricity; we don't know what it *is*, but we know what it *does*. It is an inherited capacity, and we cannot increase our share of it by our own efforts. Intelligence can be roughly measured both in children and adults.

Psychologists have given many definitions of intelligence, none of which is wholly satisfactory. For example:

(a) Intelligence is what helps human beings to adapt themselves to their environment.

This is true, but so do our instincts and emotions.

(b) Intelligence is what enables an individual to learn.

This also is true, but so do several other human capacities.

(c) Intelligence is the ability to see relationships between objects and ideas and to apply these relationships to new but similar objects and ideas.

This rather complicated definition takes us further and is probably the best definition for our purposes.

By thinking of all three definitions we should be able to grasp what intelligence does.

*Intelligence Tests.* Intelligence can be measured with moderate accuracy. Psychologists have produced tests to measure how intelligent a child is *quite separately from what he knows*. These tests are rather like puzzles. Before they are finally used, they have been tested for accuracy on thousands of children in order to discover what standard of intelligence a child should have attained at each year of his mental growth. Thus at year 8 an average child is expected to attain a standard lower than an average child of 10. The marks obtained in the test give a child's *mental age*, which may be higher or lower than his *chronological age*. In order to obtain what is called the *Intelligence Quotient*, (I.Q.) which indicates the child's intelligence, the mental age has to be related to the chronological age. This I.Q. is calculated by dividing the Mental Age by the Chronological Age, and multiplying by 100 in order to avoid the decimal points. Thus:

$$I.Q. = \frac{\text{Mental Age}}{\text{Chronological Age}} \times 100$$

For example:

Child A.  $\frac{8 \cdot 0}{10 \cdot 0} \times 100 =$ I.Q. of 80

Child B.  $\frac{12 \cdot 0}{10 \cdot 0} \times 100 =$ I.Q. of 120

Child C.  $\frac{9 \cdot 0}{9 \cdot 0} \times 100 =$ I.Q. of 100

Child A. therefore is well below the average for his age; Child B. is well above this average; Child C. is average for his age. Put in another way, Child A. has a mental age of 8 although he is 10; Child B. has a mental age of 12 although he is 10; and Child C.'s mental age corresponds with his chronological age.

An I.Q. of 100 has been chosen for the average I.Q. after tens of thousands of test experiments in Europe and America. Hence all scores over 100 indicate intelligence above average; all scores below 100 indicate intelligence below average. An I.Q. of over 120 suggests intelligence likely to carry a person through the university; a score of 80 means that the person is of very low mental ability.

There are certain points about intelligence and intelligence testing that should be noted:
1. Intelligence increases fairly steadily until the age of 16 and then further development slowly ceases, but may go on to 20.
2. Intelligence tests of the kind described measure what we may call *general* intelligence, not special types of intelligence such as those described in the next section.
3. The actual results of testing may be influenced by the state of

health or by the physical and emotional environment in which a child lives. Such causes may make a difference of ten points in the I.Q.

4. It should not be assumed that high intelligence makes certain success in studies or in a career. As we have seen, temperamental qualities like perseverance and stability of character will determine how well intelligence is used.

5. There is one last point which has special importance for any scheme of intelligence testing in Africa. This is the fact that tests used in one culture are not usually true tests in another. For example, tests used for American or European children are not good tests for African children. To get accurate tests for African children it is necessary to build up a series of tests based on lengthy experiments within the African social setting. This is being done. The methods are the same; but the subject matter of the tests is often quite different.

### Differences in Special Aptitudes

Intelligence enters into all forms of human activity. The fisherman, the carpenter, the doctor, the teacher, the motor-car mechanic, the mathematician, the architect and builder, cannot succeed in their trade unless they use their general intelligence. But in addition to their general intelligence they also have special abilities which enable them to excel in their profession. It is wrong to think that a person who is unintelligent will be better with his hands than an intelligent person. General intelligence helps all activities. Nevertheless, during adolescence, and even earlier, special aptitudes begin to appear which teachers should be most careful to notice and to encourage. They are likely to form a foundation for a pupil's career in life.

Teachers know quite well that children differ in their ability to succeed in various subjects. A pupil good at language may be weak in arithmetic; another may be good in the workshop but not good at verbal expression. The following are special aptitudes to be seen in almost any class of thirty children:

1. A high ability to remember.
2. Verbal aptitude, i.e. ability in using words and in acquiring a good vocabulary.
3. Mathematical aptitude, i.e. natural ability to calculate and see the relationship between numbers.
4. Mechanical aptitude, i.e. aptness in dealing with tools and machines; for example, the boy mechanic who sees quickly how things work and can repair a bicycle in half the time the teacher can.

5. Spatial aptitude, i.e. capacity to see the relationships of size, shape, form and thickness to any given problem. Here is the builder and architect in the making.
6. Manual aptitude, involving skill with hands such as is seen in the good carpenter, metal-worker, dress-maker, wood-carver.
7. Musical aptitude, i.e. special gifts in accuracy of tone and rhythm combined with love of music.
8. Artistic aptitude—in drawing, painting, modelling.

There are three important characteristics of these special aptitudes that should be noted. In each case, children are not only naturally skilful in these different ways, but love using their special aptitude and developing higher abilities in it. Secondly, these aptitudes are not likely to appear in children unless they have the opportunity of using them in home and school. Many a promising artist is lost in the African bush or in a school which does not care about the artistic genius of children. Thirdly, these talents, unless so strong that they are irrepressible, may die if children are ridiculed or prevented from practising them.

It may reasonably be asked why, if the growth of general intelligence ceases at the end of adolescence, it is possible for men and women in later life to show great intellectual power in special ways—the scientist, the philosopher, the mathematician, for example. This is because the adolescent has hardly begun to use the intelligence he possesses. Further study, greater knowledge and experience, and the exercise of the mind in problem-solving, steadily increase the powers of the intellect. That is why good education, and the continuing desire to educate ourselves, are so important.

The encouragement at school of the special aptitudes children develop in childhood and adolescence is an essential foundation for this development of special abilities in later life. The primary school curriculum should be such as to capture children's interests and aptitudes over a wide range of possibilities, not only in language and literature, arithmetic, history and geography, but also in art, handicraft and music. Especially is it important to develop practical abilities by providing such materials as wood, cardboard, paper, for the children to use both freely and under guidance. The same process should continue in the secondary and technical schools, especially in Africa where increasing industrialization demands many more people with mechanical skills. These skills have to be discovered early if they are to receive proper training.

## Readiness for Learning

We have noted that intelligence develops throughout childhood and that interests and aptitudes change as children grow into adolescence. It is also true that *the ability of children to perform certain tasks and to learn certain subjects depends on their stage of development*. We do not set a child of 5 to ride a bicycle, or a child of 10 to drive a motor-car. They are not physically or mentally ready to do this. The same principle applies to the learning of school subjects. There are stages in the growth of intelligence that decide at what mental age a child can learn to read and write, when he should learn to multiply and divide, or when it is possible for him to understand political history or economic geography. It is useless to teach a subject before a child is of the mental age to understand it. It is also dangerous because failure to learn will discourage him and make him less able to learn when the right time comes. When he is ready for a new stage of learning a pupil will learn quickly. Hence teachers should know what subjects to teach children at different ages. It is not always easy to know this, and pupils vary in readiness according to their mental age as distinct from their chronological age. But it is important to realize that children cannot learn what they are mentally not ready to learn. This is the main reason why it is a mistake of parents to demand nursery schools in order to teach children to read and write and calculate before they go to primary school (see page 37).

### Observation and Practical Work

1. Make notes of any special aptitudes you have observed in the children of a class in the demonstration school.
2. Make notes of any temperamental differences you have noticed in the children observed on teaching practice.
3. Make a list of five special aptitudes in older children and state for what kind of occupation they will be useful.

### Discussion and Essays

1. Explain 'intelligence' in your own words. Give examples of intelligence at work (a) in your own life, (b) in children you have taught.
2. What is meant by 'readiness to learn'? Why is it important in educating children?

# VIII

# THE GROWTH OF PERSONALITY AND CHARACTER

We conclude these chapters on 'growing up' by studying the growth of personality and character. In this way we bring together all we have learnt about childhood and adolescence. Many educational thinkers and many parents and teachers regard the development of personality and character as the chief aim of education.

Personality and character are not quite the same thing, although they are very closely allied. The word 'personality' is used to describe the kind of person we are. Every one of us has a personality quite different from all other personalities. This personality is partly inherited from our parents, especially our physical appearance. But 'the kind of person we are' is the product of all our experiences from the day we are born. One side of our personality belongs to our private life, to our innermost thoughts and feelings; it is our *inner self*, the essential ME. The other side belongs to our social life, and it is this side of us that our friends see. What we call an all-round or balanced personality is one in which the whole person has achieved harmony between his inner life and his social life.

Character is rather different. When we think of a person's character, we have in mind certain moral qualities. Character, then, is the moral side of personality. And in the development of character we aim to produce good moral qualities in a person, like courage, truthfulness, self-confidence, self-discipline, reliability. But when we aim to develop personality we hope to produce a balanced growth of the whole person; that is to say, the development not only of his moral powers but also of his body, his mind, his intellectual and artistic gifts, and of all those personal characteristics that influence his attitudes to other people.

We have already seen how children grow from one stage to another. First there is the infant stage of uncontrolled impulse during which children learn by trial and error and are closely controlled by their mother. In the second stage of childhood they learn more self-control, but parents still have to guide their unruly impulses. Nevertheless they are gradually becoming more able to control themselves and to use their freedom sensibly. The adolescent, we noted, is able to use his freedom still more profitably, because greater maturity enables him to use more self-control over his desires.

The task of parents and teachers is to help young people to pass easily from one stage to another. Just as a mother weans her baby so that he can take stronger food, so have teachers to wean children from dependence on external control to the stage of responsibility and self-control. Thus personality and character develop as children learn to control their impulses and become steady reliable persons (see Chapters XVI and XVII).

### Influences that Help the Growth of Personality and Character

In order to simplify a very complicated subject, I intend to give a list of influences that help to make us the people we are. It is a list especially useful for teachers for it reminds us of things that we have to do, and conditions that should exist, if boys and girls are to grow up into *whole persons*.

The list is rather a long one; and it leaves something to the reader's imagination because there are not many examples. It would be an excellent exercise to provide examples for all the statements made below.

We are helped to grow into a stable personality:
1. By inheriting a sound body and preserving bodily fitness by healthy living.
2. By being loved by our parents, for here is the foundation of our emotional security.
3. Through the influence of good family traditions of courage,

honesty, loyalty, social service—for these provide standards of conduct from an early age and have a lasting influence on the young.

4. By living in the right surroundings. For example: the clean, orderly and loving home; the school in which good equipment, good taste and good companionship are equally present; the helpful neighbour and the healthy and interesting neighbourhood.

5. By learning good habits. These are the foundations of reliable conduct. We *begin* to behave properly when we have acquired the habit of obedience. Pestalozzi, the lover of freedom, said that a child *needs* to learn to obey. Even while rejecting a command a child will instinctively know that obedience helps him.

6. By learning the skills of hand and eye and acquiring knowledge. Such skills and knowledge reduce our helplessness (which is the mark of infancy), and open up new worlds of activity and discovery, of *struggle* and *achievement* which are the main influences in forming character.

7. By being successful, because success gives us confidence and leads to further success.

8. By making mistakes. There is not much future for a man who does not learn from his mistakes. It is an essential part of experience.

9. By encouragement from our elders. This is the faith in us expressed by people we respect. It restores the tired will and is a stimulus to greater effort (see page 99).

10. By living with the right people—in our home, school and neighbourhood—because the people we mix with form our opinions and influence our conduct (see page 9).

11. By admiring the right people, because we tend to become like those we admire. We are bound to go where we are looking!

12. By accepting the customs and rules which train us in good manners and courtesy. This is social education, because it requires us to respect the rights and feelings of others. And, by this limitation of our desire to do as we like, we learn self-discipline (see page 95).

13. By co-operating with others in home, school and village so that we learn how to work with other people. This, too, is essential social experience. Man cannot live alone. He must co-operate with his fellow men or live a less than human existence.

14. By obeying our elders. This is the external discipline which helps us to behave before we are morally strong enough to control ourselves (see page 95).

15. By obeying ourselves. This is the self-discipline that enables us to exercise control over our desires without the discipline of our elders. We are good when no one is watching us (see page 95).

16. By accepting responsibility. This is the chief means of acquiring confidence in ourselves and the most important way of building a stable character (see page 96).

17. By having ideals. To have an ideal is to unite all our energies, disciplines, knowledge and skills in the pursuit of a good purpose. It is to have a goal to aim at. The influence of an ideal in building personality is explained in the following paragraph.

All living things aim at wholeness, to be complete, perfect. This is a law of nature. Every plant, tree, animal or human being strives for wholeness. Prune the branch of a tree and it grows more branches; cut your finger and it will heal with little help from you. This wholeness of the body we call *physical health*. When all urges, desires and abilities work together in harmony we have *wholeness of personality*. It is when we are thus fully engaged in the pursuit of a goal that our personality is built up. That is why ideals are important.

It is in the home and in schools that ideals are formed. Hence great responsibility rests on parents and teachers to see that young people acquire healthy ideals. These ideals can be of many kinds; some are very simple and some difficult to achieve. In primary school they can be as simple as ideals of neatness and punctuality. Later on the goal we set for ourselves may be success in a school subject or in a hobby, or success in a particular career. These smaller ideals may later develop into really big ideals which take a life-time to achieve. For example, we may be willing to use all our energies and skills to serve the community as teacher or doctor, or give up wealth to serve the poor and the sick. And because they are ideals they make use of all our capacities and continue to build up personality and character.

Thus we arrive at the conclusion that the makers of character and personality are our homes, our schools and ourselves.

### Observation and Practical Work

1. On pages 52 to 54 there is a list of influences that help to form personality and character. Give examples or illustrations of each one—if possible from your own experience.

**Discussion and Essays**
1. What is the difference between personality and character?
2. The influence of 'purpose' on the formation of character. Give examples of various kinds of purpose (a) in children, (b) in adolescents.

# PART III

# LEARNING

# IX

# PERCEIVING

First note that the word giving the title to this chapter is a verb. That is to say it is a word expressing *activity*. We could have used the noun 'perception', but a noun does not sufficiently emphasize the idea of activity. We shall have to use the noun frequently in what follows in this chapter, but we must think of it always as a word that describes what people do. We perceive almost every moment of the day. If we did not we should be less than half alive.

Obviously, then, perceiving is important. It is indeed the most important single activity of human beings. Without perception we could not learn; we could not act; we could not think; we should have nothing to remember; we could imagine nothing in our minds; we should not understand what our senses were trying to tell us. It is by applying our intelligence to the impressions made on one or more of our senses that we are able to perceive. We are able to perceive millions of things without training, but there are some things we can only perceive clearly by learning how to perceive them. Thus perception assists learning; and we can also learn to perceive.

What do we do when we perceive? In effect we transform impressions made upon our senses by the objects and people or events around us, into *awareness* of those objects, people and events. A small child perceives his mother, that is he is *aware* of her, when he sees her, hears her, or feels her. Thus this instance of perception involves seeing, hearing, feeling but *also* previous experience of his mother. If, for example, he were sitting under a mango tree at play and his mother approached from behind, very quietly so that he could not hear her movements, then he would not perceive her even though she were only a yard away. But if she whispered his name in the voice he knew so well, he would perceive her without seeing her. Immediately the mother's voice would bring together other memories of 'mother' and he would be aware of her, and could see her in his 'mind's eye' before she stood before him in the flesh.

A good deal of special knowledge and skill are required in the more complicated acts of perceiving. Consider two men, one an African hunter and tracker, with a life-long experience of the bush and forest and of the habits of wild animals; the other a motor-engineer who had always lived in the city. Suppose each, in turn, takes the other into his own sphere of experience—the hunter guides the engineer in a hunting expedition; the engineer takes the hunter to the city in his car. Each is equally intelligent, equally good in hearing and vision. The hunter will perceive a leopard in a tree where the engineer sees only leaves and branches; a herd of buck on the horizon where the engineer sees bushes and rocks; the cry of a heron where the engineer merely hears a queer noise. The hunter has *perceived* many exciting objects of which the engineer was unaware.

Now suppose the engineer takes the hunter to the city in his car. The positions are reversed. From a pull on the steering wheel the engineer would perceive that one front tyre was flat; an unusual noise in the engine would warn him of trouble. All the time he wa driving he would be receiving sense impressions—sight, hearing, touch, smell —that would enable him to perceive a hundred happenings to his car such as speed, smoothness of running and so on, and also conditions on the road that affected his driving. All of these impressions he would interpret according to his previous experience of motor-cars. Few of these things would the hunter even notice. Each man received stimuli—the leopard, the engine noise—each paid attention to the stimulus of which he was aware; but not to the stimulus outside his experience.

If we examine these examples of perception we shall discover the means by which we perceive.
(a) There must be a stimulus from the senses.
(b) This stimulus must be understood.

(c) The stimulus must have a colour, shape, pattern; a tone of sound, or quality of taste or smell.
(d) Perception may depend on previous experience of the object perceived (e.g. the child's perception of his mother).
(e) Perception depends on separating out what is being perceived from its surroundings i.e. it depends on distinguishing between the object and what surrounds it, e.g. the leopard from the tree.
(f) Perception can be learned.
(g) Perception requires attention.

Briefly then, we receive impressions through our senses; these impressions stimulate memory of similar experiences; our mind connects the old with the new; and thus perception takes place.

It would be possible to give much more complicated examples of perception which would indicate that the objects of perception may include not only objects we can see or hear or touch, but events and abstract qualities like height and breadth; even the moods and temperament of persons. If we turn back to Chapter V for example, we should realize that all the inborn tendencies of children there mentioned are actually to be perceived by the teacher. Thus it is a great mistake to think that perceiving deals only with material objects. In fact perception ranges from the simple objects perceived by babies to perceptions of complicated events, and problems resulting from wide knowledge and experience in adult life. In all school activities perception plays a large part; it is involved in reading and writing, in the learning of all school subjects, in games, and in our attitudes to people in school.

### The Improving of Perceiving

Anyone watching a baby at play will observe that the baby is perceiving all kinds of objects without any assistance. But as perceiving is so important in education it is one of the teacher's tasks to improve the perceptual capacities of children, both by creating good habits of perceiving and by training them to perceive the important aspects of a school subject. In effect our object is to enable children to use efficiently their natural capacity for perceiving—to have eyes that see and ears that hear. The following ways are suggested for improving children's powers of perception. Note how closely these methods are allied to those suggested in the chapter dealing with curiosity, construction and play. Indeed it would be useful at this point to re-read Chapter V before proceeding.

1. Young children should be free to explore their surroundings, to

handle, feel, taste, smell and play with objects in home and school—toys, blocks, cans, paper, water, pets, flowers. To splash in water, to feel the smoothness of a stone, the softness of a dog's coat, the coolness of mud and the rough fluidity of sand, to smell the fragrance of a flower—these experiences sharpen perception. And to give *names* to objects perceived enriches the meaning of the perception. Always, try then, to attach a name to objects and sensations—pot, flower, smooth, rough, hot, cold, etc.

2. Select objects and materials which are likely to encourage interests you have already observed in children. Produce models, pictures, diagrams that draw attention to the important details of colour, shape, and the relationship of one part to another. Examples of these would be models for the teaching of number, relief maps and the sand tray for use in geography, pictures in rural science and health education. In all types of teaching ask questions that direct a pupil's attention to details that may have escaped his attention; and also test their observation by getting them to write descriptions of what they have observed. This especially applies to field excursions and pictures where children's attention can easily wander outside the range of what is to be observed. Drawing pictures of things observed is a specially good way of stimulating careful observation.

There is a story told of a student in a biology class at a university which illustrates the importance of observing. It was his first day. His professor threw a dead fish on to the bench and told him to make a list of all the things he had observed about the fish. In an hour he came back with about ten items on his list. 'Spend two more hours really looking', the professor said. The student this time had a longer list. 'Spend all afternoon on it,' said the professor. Sadly the student went back to his task; but each time the number of items on his list grew. The next day, and the next, the heartless professor sent his pupil back to observe more detail. The trial went on for two weeks, at the end of which the list of observed characteristics had reached nearly 1,000. 'Now you know something about a fish', said the professor. The student had 'perceived' a fish. Perhaps it should be added that this student one day became a professor. The lesson in this story must not be misunderstood. It is intended to indicate the immense value of careful observation. We cannot make such demands on children; but we can insist on, say, five minutes observation perhaps under the stimulus of competition, e.g. 'See who can discover most interesting things about this coconut (banana, map) in five minutes'.

3. Perception plays an important part in speech and in acquiring the language skills of reading and writing. Correct perception in speech involves careful pronunciation on the part of the teacher and accurate listening on the part of the pupil. The child learns the spoken word first. He has to bridge the gap between the word he hears and the written word he sees, i.e. the written form has to have the same meaning for him as the spoken form. This will not happen easily unless the spoken word is pronounced clearly and unless the written word is written clearly; and *also* unless the child perceives differences between words that are similar in appearance. Reading and writing are speeded up if a child's perceptions of sound and sight are made sharp and clear; they are retarded if perceptions are vague. The teacher, then, must help him to observe the differences between similar words, e.g. between *now* and *mow*, *sow* and *sew*, *hot* and *dot*. The teacher will also write legibly and speak slowly and clearly—thus appealing to the sensations both of sight and hearing.

4. Perceiving involves *attending*. Although many people think they can attend to many things at one time, in fact they can only attend to one thing at a time. We can shift our attention quickly from one thing to another, like the business man with six telephones on his desk. But we can't read a novel under the desk and fully attend to the history lesson. We can pay attention to a banana plant or to a banana plantation, but not to both at the same time. We can pay attention to a banana leaf or to a banana plant, but not to both simultaneously.

We attend best when we are *interested*. Hence when a teacher wishes his pupils to perceive clearly he must secure their interest. A child is interested when he feels that what is to be observed is something that he wants to know more about. It is a desire within him that demands satisfaction. This desire can be strengthened by stirring his curiosity and wonder. Hence teachers should know what children are interested in, so that they can appeal to interests already awakened in their pupils. Here again we have to refer to the inborn tendencies in children. It is from these that interests arise, and it is to these that the teacher must appeal.

But in the classroom attention may have to be secured immediately in order that work may proceed. We have, therefore, to provide the right kind of stimulus to attention. Such a stimulus should have the following characteristics: it should be *vivid*—bright colours for younger children, bold clear diagrams for older children. It should 'catch the eye'. For this reason *movement* is arresting—models that *work*. It should stand out clearly from its background—a diagram on an untidy blackboard will not do; an object on a crowded desk will not be well perceived because attention will be scattered.

An ingenious teacher will have great fun in devising methods of securing attention in these ways. But he should also remember that in his *voice* he has a splendid means for securing attention if it is not used too much. This flexible instrument can give colour and novelty to a story he is telling, to a demonstration on the bench or on the blackboard. Too many teachers use the voice only to *order* children to attend—Listen! Look! Children will not attend for long if the command is followed by a colourless talk empty of real interest for them. Why should they? Attention has to be maintained as well as secured for a few minutes. The secrets of maintaining attention are active and interested children, vivid presentation of lessons, and a teacher who knows that he can sharpen the children's perceptual powers during the process of learning.

### Observation and Practical Work

1. Place a large picture before the class. Tell the children to make a list of all the things they see. Compare the results with your own observation of the picture and also note the differences in the children's results. How do you account for these differences?
2. Place ten different objects on a table and ask the children, in groups of not more than 15 at a time, to look at them carefully. After five minutes cover up the objects and tell the children to write down the names of as many as they can remember. Play the same game with some of your fellow students but using twenty objects.
3. Make lists of the different ways of using ALL the children's interests and abilities, (a) in learning to read in Class I, (b) in learning multiplication in Class II, (c) in nature study in Class III, (d) in geography in Class IV.

### Discussion and Essays

1. The relation between good observation and good perception.
2. How can the voice be used to increase attention?
3. How can classroom exhibitions be used to increase perception, (a) in history, (b) in nature study?

# X
# THINKING, CONCEPTS AND IMAGINATION

We have noted that we cannot remember, think or learn without perceiving. We have also noted that in perceiving we have to do a little thinking. The baby under the mango tree was beginning to think. The hunter and the motor engineer were doing more complicated thinking. But in each case the thinking was stimulated by events that were actually being *seen* or *heard at the time*. This is the starting point of thinking. But it does not take us far enough. A more advanced and complicated form of thinking is necessary to solve the kind of problem which faces us when the concrete image—mother, the leopard, the car noise—is not present. In other words we have to think about the 'ideas' of things. And ideas exist only in the mind.

We give the name *concept* to the pattern of ideas we build up around an object or idea with which we are familiar. We build up these patterns in our own minds. Here is a simple example: a child sees a dog. He sees another dog. To *him* each dog is *a* dog. As he grows older he sees lots and lots of dogs, all different, but all dogs. Gradually he realizes that they all have certain characteristics in common—four legs, a warm hairy coat, a tail, and also what we can only call 'dogginess'. He has formed in his mind a general idea of 'dog'. This is his pattern or *concept* of 'dog'. The more he comes to know about dogs, the more contact he has with them, with cattle dogs, house dogs, big dogs, little dogs, hunting dogs, the fuller his concept of 'dog' will be. He will soon reach a stage of mental development when this concept of dogs will enable him to think about dogs *when he is not looking at a dog*. He has gradually accumulated a 'bundle' of images, feelings and ideas which together form a pattern of 'dogginess'.

This process of forming concepts goes on throughout life. In childhood, we form simple concepts of concrete and living things—houses, animals, trees, bicycles. As we grow older and our special interests develop, we go on forming more complicated concepts until we acquire not only ideas about dogs but ideas about ideas. Thus, for example, we may accumulate patterns of ideas about parents, school, football, arithmetic, examinations, and also about honesty and fairplay. As citizens we gradually develop political or social concepts and build up ideas about freedom, justice and democracy.

These concepts are at the same time a result of our thinking and learning and also one of the means by which we continue to learn. For it must be obvious that the bigger the bundle of ideas we have accumulated around any topic, the more are we able to learn about it. We have more points from which to start our thinking about it. If I asked an African boy of fifteen who Alexander the Great was he might not be able to answer. If I asked the same question of a Professor of History, his answer might fill a book. We should expect the Chief Justice to know more about justice than a child of ten, because his concept of 'justice' would be immensely richer in content. We should expect a teacher to have a better concept of 'education' than his pupils or their parents. But this should not be taken for granted. Some parents know more about education than some teachers because they have studied their own children with understanding and entered into their games and interests. The parent who so enters into his children's lives will acquire a rich concept of childhood.

*Language* is most important in forming concepts because words provide a label for any concept we have formed. A label helps to separate one object or idea from another object or idea. The word 'cube' describes what a cube is as distinct from a square; the word 'tree' marks a distinction between tree and flower; the word 'mango' separates a mango tree from all other trees. *Thus words help us to get clear concepts.* But if a child sees or hears a word which describes a concept which he has not formed, he will not understand the meaning of the word, and therefore will not get the full meaning of the sentence which contains the unknown word. If, for example, you say to a child of ten 'I want you to acquire a clear concept of the geological structure of a mountain', he will not understand you. If you say 'I want you to get a clear picture in your mind of this mountain', he probably will. This is because he has no concept of 'geology' and no concept of 'structure'.

Because we are able to think we are able to form concepts; because we can form concepts we are able to think better. But thinking is essential to another mental activity. Thinking helps us to *solve problems*—from the simplest problem in arithmetic to building an aeroplane. Hence we can now say this about human thought: thinking depends on using what we have perceived, remembering facts we have learned, using concepts we have formed, *and being faced with a problem*.

### Problem solving

If then we wish to improve children's thinking (and our own) we have to face them with problems. Several principles should govern our choice and presentation of a problem:

(a) It should as far as possible be presented in a form appealing to a child's interests. For younger children practical problems of construction are excellent for this purpose, e.g. 'make a bridge out of these ten blocks of wood'.

(b) It should not be too hard for a child of the right age, but hard enough to make him strive a little before its solution.

(c) The statement of the problem should be in words the child can understand.

In order to solve a problem, a child must have some data to work on, that is, facts that are given, in order to discover by *reasoning* the answer to the problem. Reasoning is the gift we have *for discovering what we do not know by thinking based on what we do know*. Here is a simple example:

*John is older than Mary; Mary is older than Jane. Who is the youngest?*

This is a very simple problem typical of a large number of problems of much greater complexity, where a number of facts have to be put in proper relation to each other before the answer appears. The solution of all problems by reasoning involves intelligence. That is why some people can solve problems better than others. A child who cannot reason at all has a very low intelligence. But we should assume that all children can reason, certainly from the time they enter infant school.

Children, especially older children, should be helped to reason clearly and not to take short cuts, i.e. come to conclusions that the facts do not justify. They must not be allowed to 'jump to conclusions'. Teachers will therefore help them to proceed cautiously; they should point out facts that have been forgotten and conclusions that are not justified by the evidence. For example, what is wrong with the following conclusion?

*Africans live in East Africa; Nairobi is in East Africa; therefore all people in Nairobi are Africans.*

## Imagination

*Imagination* is another help to thinking and learning. This is an activity of the mind which enables us to form two kinds of mental pictures or images:

1. Mind-pictures, or images, of *past events*, i.e. of things that have already happened to us. These are mental images called to mind by the use of our memory.

This type of remembering through mind-pictures is best called *imaging*, i.e. the creation of images of events, things or persons *we have seen before*.

2. The mind can also construct, build up, quite new images by combining old ideas and old mental images to form patterns of thinking and behaviour *for the future*. This is a most remarkable and wonderful capacity that we all possess. And, note, it is a capacity that can be improved with practice and training.

This kind of imagining is best called *imagination*, which is one of the most precious mental capacities of human beings and the source of much progress in human thought. The remarkable thing that happens in imagination is that we *create something new*, that never existed before. The best examples of this creative thinking are the discoveries of the scientist, the writings of the novelist and poet and the musical composer.

Simple examples of *imaging* and *imagination* will help to make clear the difference between these two mental activities. First note that there is nothing unusual about forming images in the mind. We all do it, almost every hour of the day. Try now to get mind-images of the following:

(a) A mango tree; your mother cooking a meal; your bicycle. These are *visual* images.
(b) The call of a bird; the sound of drums; the howling of a dog. These are *sound* images.
(c) A game of football; legs pedalling a bicycle; people dancing. These are images of *movement*.
(d) The feel of a road under bare feet; of a banana skin; of water and soap when washing the hands. These are images of *touch*.
(e) The smell of dinner cooking; of an orange; of paraffin oil. These are images of *smell*.
(f) The taste of salt; of fish; of your favourite drink. These are images of *taste*.

Note that in all this 'imaging' we are using our memory of past experiences. But how can we imagine the future?

I shall now attempt to give an example of the *imagination* at work by using a situation which every teacher will have to imagine quite frequently. Here it is:

You have to prepare a lesson for the next day. You have planned it in your note book and decided what you are going to teach, the facts and their order of presentation, the illustrations you are going to use. But so far all this is in your note book and it won't be of much use if it stays there. Now imagine yourself in the actual classroom; with the actual children, the familiar blackboard, your material for illustration on the table. See the children; see their faces and the whites of their eyes; see them listening; see yourself giving out illustrative material; see your neat diagrams on the blackboard; feel the chalk in your hand; hear the tones of your voice as you explain this or that, or call a child to attention; listen to their questions and to your answers; see them at work after you have set them to draw, paint, write, do their sums. And so on. See yourself doing your teaching.

Now none of this has happened! It is a picture of *tomorrow*, which you have deliberately produced in your mind to help you to give a good lesson. I, who am writing it, have done the same piece of imagining in order to write the above paragraph. I can at the moment of writing see all this happening quite clearly—in my imagination. I have even imagined you and the boys and girls and the open window. It is raining. Both you and I have performed a most complicated mental activity which has brought together dozens of people and things in one whole by an effort of imagination. *We have imagined a good lesson.* And when this has been done the real lesson will be a better one than if its preparation had remained a few notes in a notebook. Better to have your notes (and pictures) in your head than your head in your notes.

Thus *imaging* helps us to remember; *imagining* helps us to create new situations. Both are important to children and teachers in learning and teaching. The fact that children can make these images involving sight, sound, movement, touch and smell, suggests that we should appeal to this image-making capacity in our teaching. We should try to apply the following methods whenever practicable:

1. Appeal to as many types of images as possible, to sight and sound in particular as these are the senses most frequently used in image-making.
2. Make our lessons as vivid and colourful as possible. They should be lively, full of life and children's activity.
3. Children should especially be encouraged to draw. *Their* visual imagery is usually strong as is shown by their imaginative drawings and paintings.
4. In such subjects as history and geography they should be helped to visualize scenes and the countryside and people they have not seen.
5. In teaching literature, readings and poems should be so chosen as to appeal to real experiences of the children. They will form better new images when these are based on images in their own memory.
6. In mathematics, and other subjects, diagrams or concrete objects should be used, made by both teacher and pupils, to illustrate the relations between number and the shape of concrete objects. Examples would be self-made models to illustrate the dimensions of a rectangular box or the movement of the earth round the sun, or to explain night and day.
7. Remember that children learn more by creating their own images i.e. by doing things for themselves, than by seeing the teacher do them and listening to explanations in words only.
8. One of the best ways to help children to use their imagination is to dramatize stories and events in history and literature.

Finally, remember that a teacher will not be able to stimulate the imagination of his pupils unless he uses his own. We can all improve our capacity to imagine if we daily use our imagination. It is only by imagination that we can understand children. We have, so to speak, to get inside their skins, to try and feel what they are feeling and see what they are seeing. We have to imagine what special difficulties they encounter in facing a problem, in grasping the meaning of a new word or a new idea. We have constantly to remember that we may use a sentence that has complete meaning for us, but may have no meaning at all for the children.

### Observation and Practical Work

1. Construct a problem that would help a child *to think* in each of the following situations: (a) for a child in Class I a problem involving the construction of a pattern out of pieces of paper, (b) for a child in Class III a problem in arithmetic, (c) for a child in Class VI a problem in nature study.
2. Prepare exercises that will help children to use their imagination, (a) in literature, (b) in history, (c) in geography, (d) in painting a picture.

### Discussion and Essays

1. Describe your own 'concept' of (a) a motor-car, (b) a school, (c) freedom, (d) honesty.
2. What is the connection between language and the forming of clear 'concepts'? Why is this connection important in teaching?
3. What is the difference between 'imaging' and 'imagination'? Give examples.

# XI

## REMEMBERING AND FORGETTING[*]

We could not learn anything if we could not remember. Good teaching helps remembering; bad teaching helps forgetting. Hence if we want our pupils to remember what they have been taught we have to make every effort to teach them by good methods. Here are some principles and methods that teachers should use if they wish their pupils to remember what they have been taught.

1. Children will remember and therefore learn best when they *want* to learn. They will not want to learn unless they are interested. They will be interested in a lesson when they see in it a means of satisfying their curiosity. Hence the teacher must stimulate their curiosity. He will do this only when he associates what he wants them to learn with their *special interests*, their *previous knowledge* and their *special aptitudes*. Children will remember best those facts that increase their knowledge of things they are interested in. Hence, in any class he is teaching, a teacher should be aware of the interests of these particular pupils. He will realize that Class I, for example, will have different interests from Class IV. In each case he will start his lesson with a reference to these particular interests.

The above paragraph could be put into one sentence: Children remember well when their whole personality is engaged in the task of learning.

---

[*]This chapter should be supplemented by Appendix I.

2. We learn and remember best when new knowledge is firmly connected to *what we already know*. We should always attach facts that are to be learned to facts that have already been learned. Thus at the beginning of a lesson we should go over the facts the pupils know of that subject before we begin to teach them what they do not know.
3. Children do not remember facts that are described in words they do not understand. Nobody does. Hence teachers should use words children can understand. If children are to learn from a book the teacher should be sure that they understand the meaning of all words they are to read. This explains the danger of too much mechanical learning by heart in which children can recite words without grasping their meaning. What is committed to memory must first be understood:
4. *Practice* in using new knowledge is essential for remembering what has been learned. When pupils have learned how to multiply and divide, for example, they should have plenty of practice in multiplying and dividing before going on to further arithmetical work. Similarly they should be given repeated practice in the use of new words in sentences both in speech and in writing.
5. *Repetition* is essential to good remembering. Teachers should be sure to make their pupils repeat what they have learned, e.g. their tables, meaning of words, poems. And, note, it is best to make these repetitions on several separate occasions, say on each of five consecutive days, than all at once in one long lesson.

There is a place in school for rhythmic chanting of tables and rules of arithmetic or spelling, for children are quick to pick up rhythm. The danger of this method is that emphasis on rhythm may obscure the meaning of what is to be learnt in this way. There is the example of children who had to learn a hymn which began

"Weak and sinful though we be . . . "
The teacher found they were singing

"we can sing, full though we be . . . "
They had got the rhythm, but not the meaning of the words. It is not easy for a teacher to know whether children are repeating wrong words when the whole class is reciting at the same time.
6. When learning by heart—e.g. passages of prose, lists of words, poems—remembering is improved by *spacing the learning*. For example, twenty lines of poetry will be learned more accurately and remembered longer if learned for ten minutes on one day and ten minutes on the next day, than if an attempt were made to learn the whole passage in one effort of twenty minutes.

7. *Frequent testing*, like frequent repetition, helps children to remember. Children should be taught to test themselves in order to discover what they have not learned. This is really a kind of repetition. All testing should be done in such a way that the children find it interesting. In other words testing should be a really educational exercise, not merely a way of discovering what a child does not know.

8. Good learning and remembering require *effort*. The more effort a child puts into learning the better he will remember what he has learnt. Repetition, testing, physical activity, all kinds of interests that make a child put his whole energy into learning, will help him to remember.

9. Obviously, from all we now know about perceiving clearly, and the importance of imagination in learning, children will remember best when they are encouraged to make *clear mental images* of the topics they have to learn. Drawing and all kinds of manual activity are therefore aids to good remembering.

10. Finally, children will not learn or remember if they are tired, or hungry, or sick or bored. A healthy body is as necessary as an alert mind for all kinds of learning. If a child has walked six miles to school on little or no breakfast, has no lunch before afternoon school, neither parents nor teachers should expect him to remember or learn anything.

### Observation and Practical Work

1. (a) Choose a short poem or three verses from the Bible. Give the class a brief lesson on its meaning. Read it aloud as well as you can. Give them ten minutes to learn it by heart and then ask them to write it out.

   (b) Choose a similar passage of the same length and give the class twenty minutes to learn it by heart without help from you. Ask them to write it out.

   Compare the results of the two methods and draw conclusions.

2. Make a collection of as many different kinds of test material as possible.

3. In your practice school (or any other school) find out how many children, (a) have had something to *eat* for breakfast, and (b) have brought lunch with them or are going to eat school lunch.

### Discussion and Essays

1. The objects of testing what children have learned.
2. In your own words say what are the main conditions necessary for good remembering.

# PART IV
# TEACHING

# XII

## THE TEACHER AS A PERSON

Teachers' Colleges, or Colleges of Education, which is a better term, will do two things:
(a) They will continue the student's personal education and help him to become a good person.
(b) They will introduce him to the difficult art of teaching, its theory and its practice.

Some people think teachers' colleges should produce fully trained teachers at the end of the course. This is not what colleges do, or claim to do. They lay foundations upon which the young teacher can build. It is during the next five or ten years of teaching that he will complete for himself what the college began to do for him. Only in school can he get the experience that counts.

BUT, experience is of no use if we are too proud to learn by it. There are millions of people in the world who have had lots of experience—but they are no wiser. So, let us remember that the amount of experience we have had is of less importance than our ability to profit by it. The best teachers are those who have the humility and capacity to learn by success and failure. Humility is the capacity to accept the criticism of others and to criticize ourselves without feeling too sorry for ourselves.

It should now be obvious to 'students in training' that a large part of their future success depends on themselves, on their knowledge, on their attitude to learning their job, on their capacity to learn by their own experience, and on the conduct of their personal lives. But none of these good things is enough in itself to make a good teacher:

*Knowledge* is not enough if we do not know how to pass it on to our pupils.

*Training* is not enough if we have no knowledge to pass on.

*Experience* is not enough unless we learn by it.

*Good character* has to be supported by knowledge and skill in the classroom.

A large part of this book is concerned with what a teacher ought to *do*. The next few paragraphs suggest what sort of person a teacher ought to *be*.

1. A teacher should be a person of *good character*—a man or woman who respects truth, who is sincere in word and act, who likes people and especially children, and whose personal life sets a good example to his pupils. He should have a sense of humour; which means that he can laugh at himself and that the children will laugh with him. These qualities of character are the solid foundation of the good teacher's work. Parents will feel that their children are safe in the care of such a person.

2. *The good teacher will remain a student all his life.* Only in this way can he become an educated person, which is what every teacher should wish to be. Teaching fails when we cease to learn, no matter how old we are. What we have learned at school and college is only the beginning of knowledge. The School Certificate is a beginning, the Teacher's Certificate is another beginning. If we have a university degree, this too is the beginning, not the end, of the journey. For these are only stages on the pathway to knowledge and wisdom. The test of the truly educated person is that he knows that he does not know all he ought to know. The mind of the man or woman who goes on learning stays alive; the mind of the person who thinks he knows all he needs to know is already dead. Our minds remain alive only if we use them. This is true whether we are merely learning new facts or whether we are thinking out new ways of teaching.

The teacher must always know far more than it is necessary for his pupils to know. He will strive to enrich his mind with new knowledge and ideas so that his teaching becomes more exciting and more attractive. Think then of the meaning of these wise words: 'The education of the pupil is always the self-education of the teacher'.

3. *The good teacher will know his world.* The teacher's world, as we saw in Chapter II, is a very wide world. It is wider than his home, wider than his classroom or his village or his native land. But his mind is the meeting place of home, school and country. By keeping in touch with what is happening in the world, with the new ideas, inventions, and with strange events that occur every day, he is able to simplify and explain them to his pupils. Thus he takes his pupils on wonderful journeys of exploration through the big world they live in. He helps them to understand what is new and puzzling to them. But he will never do this if his mind is confined between the covers of a text-book.

4. *The good teacher will have a special interest.* Most teachers have to teach several subjects; but we cannot know all of them equally well. Nothing gives us more confidence than knowing one subject really well. We should try to become expert in something that really interests us. The choice is without limit—the history or geography of our country, its traditions and songs. Or it may be farming, carpentry or cooking, birds, flowers, insects. There is much for African teachers to do to record the local names of animals, birds, flowers and trees before they disappear for ever. It is sad to think that the vernacular names for this permanent part of our environment are being forgotten. Some teachers will strive to excel in some part of physical education; others may make themselves experts in some special form of teaching method. When pupils discover an enthusiast in the school some of them will soon catch his enthusiasm.

5. *The good teacher will know his pupils as well as his teaching subjects.* So much has been said already on this topic that no more need be said here.

6. *The good teacher will be adaptable.* If our education has been of any use it will have given us the initiative to tackle new jobs at short notice. We must be willing to face and to solve new problems—practical problems like teaching a subject we did not learn at college, or building a cycle shed with the pupils' help, or cooking dinner because the cook is ill, or cleaning up the classroom after a flood, or managing the school in the Head's absence.

7. There are situations when adaptability has to be combined with *courage.*

You may be faced in your first job with bad school conditions—a poor building, a leaking roof, dark classrooms, no cupboards for materials, your books eaten by termites, no wall-space for pictures.

Here is a tremendous challenge to the young teacher's adaptability and imagination—'Shall I run away; or shall I fight back and improve my teaching conditions by my own efforts?'

Thousands of young men and women have faced these enemies of education. They have fought and won. And the struggle has tremendously strengthened them as teachers and human beings. But it takes courage to keep going. Four things help us to go on:

(a) Getting results: e.g. in making a cupboard for materials; then a place for wall pictures and so on.
(b) The assistance and co-operation of our pupils.
(c) Keeping our minds at work by reading and hobbies and by cultivating our special interests. This keeps us in touch with the world outside school.
(d) Preserving contact with our college and getting its support.
(e) Attending refresher courses that keep us alive to new possibilities, and bring us into contact with people facing similar difficulties.

Our motto then will be: *It is my job to turn adversity into opportunity.*

Without pupils there would be no schools. Without teachers there would be no schools. Parents provide the children; teachers provide the essential service that makes their education possible. In school, then, *the teacher is the most important part of the children's environment.* He controls the materials and methods of learning. He decides how the children live and work and play together. He decides how his pupils use their physical environment in the school and in the neighbourhood (see page 19). And all the time he is with his pupils he is exchanging ideas with them, helping them to think, forming their minds, setting an example, guiding their moral understanding. Thus he sets the *tone* of the whole school community.

This is surely a task that raises the teacher to the highest level of importance in any community. So there are very good reasons why teachers should have a deep respect for their profession.

### The Teacher's Attitudes

Our attitude to a person is our feeling towards him. When we speak of a teacher's attitude to his pupils, or the pupils' attitude to him, we refer to the almost unconscious feelings they have when they meet or think of each other. These feelings are important for good classroom and school relationships. They may be feelings of respect and friendliness, or feelings of scorn or resentment. In school these attitudes are largely due to the feelings a teacher has for his pupils, because the attitudes of the children tend to reflect the attitudes of the teacher. A class whose teacher is friendly and courteous is likely to be friendly and well-mannered. A class whose teacher shouts and bullies will be misbehaved and resentful. In the former case the class will co-operate willingly because they feel their teacher is working *with* them. In the second case pupils will not easily co-operate because they feel their teacher is *against* them.

This relationship between a teacher and his pupils can be described in another way. If we think of the class as a circle, then good relationships and good work require that the teacher and his pupils are all *inside* the circle. But if the teacher always stays *outside* the circle, then relationships will not be so good because teacher and children are not working together. The teacher and pupils should all feel themselves to be inside the same circle. Then it becomes a circle of sympathy and understanding which binds them all together.

A teacher should be able to look at his class on the first day of term and say to himself: '*I am on your side.*' When the children know that 'he is on our side', the circle of understanding is complete. The teacher may lose his temper occasionally, he may at times be severe, he may make them work hard. But when the children know he is always on their side they will accept all kinds of correction with a good heart. This will not happen with a teacher who is 'always against them.'

There are several ways in which teachers can build up this good relationship which inspires the children's confidence.

1. There is *the way of speech:* the friendly voice, the calm deliberate speech which makes instructions clear; the word of warning that demands good behaviour without bad tempered threats. The teacher who shouts will find the children shouting too; the teacher who talks too much will be holding up class activity. Such teachers will irritate. The loud voice should be used rarely if it is to have effect. Only the good story-teller should talk for more than ten minutes at a time. Remember, the children must talk too.

2. Pay *attention to individuals*. The bond between children and their teacher is strengthened when children feel he is interested in their success and failure. When children are at work individually or in groups, give a helping hand where it is needed.

3. *Encourage* rather than condemn. Encouragement has been proved to bring better results than punishment.

4. Treat misbehaviour or difficulties in learning as *problems to be*

*solved by you as an expert.* Do not regard them as attempts to annoy you. The doctor called in to a case of measles is not personally offended because the child has been so foolish as to catch the disease. He looks for the symptoms and decides on the proper treatment. That is what the good teacher will do. His treatment may be kind or it may have to be severe and painful. But the culprit is more likely to accept it if he knows that 'teacher is on my side'.

5. *Do not be afraid of not knowing* the answer to a child's question. This is no disgrace; it is an opportunity for good teaching. We cannot know all the answers. I have seen so many young teachers who did not know the answer stammering away trying to appear as if they did know. This way they lose the confidence of the class. Just say 'I don't know; but let's find out'. And there you have another good lesson provided for you.

I remember an occasion many years ago when as a young teacher I was being inspected by one of His Majesty's Inspectors: a very intelligent boy asked a question in our class discussion and I said 'I don't know, but I can tell you where you can find out. Bring us the answer tomorrow'. To my surprise, the inspector came to me at the end of the lesson and said 'You know, that was the best part of the lesson, when you said you didn't know'. The moral is that children will forgive occasional ignorance, but will not forgive the teacher who tries to hide ignorance in many words.

A great Oxford teacher once said to his students, 'Don't look at me; look where I am looking.' Here was one of the greatest scholars of his time humbly standing within the circle of learning, alongside those who knew so little. He did not say 'I have the knowledge you want. Just look at me and listen.' His object was to turn their gaze in the right direction so that *together* they might make discoveries. This is the attitude of the good teacher towards his pupils and their learning.

### The Importance of Method

This is not a book about teaching methods. Your college will give you instruction in the art of teaching, which, like all arts, can only be learnt by teaching under the guidance of skilled tutors. This is the most essential help the college can give to the young teacher.

Consider the conditions the new teacher faces in his first job. He joins a school whose staff he does not know. He is confronted with boys and girls he has never seen before, whose homes and background are unknown to him. He has still to discover the characters and abilities of his pupils, and this will take many months. But he knows that he has to start teaching them *tomorrow*. This is not an easy task he faces. His great need is *confidence*. And nothing will provide this confidence so well as a firm grasp of a few teaching methods that he has himself proved to be workable.

The following points should be borne in mind when any method is being used:

1. A method is the practical application of good teaching principles, based on the nature of children, the nature of the subject and the learning needs of the pupils.
2. The object of any teaching method is to ensure effective learning.
3. All methods are useless unless the teacher knows his subject.
4. All methods of teaching must provide for good class management, e.g. interest, attention, the children's activity and good order.
5. The teacher should never be so concerned with his 'method' as to forget his pupils. The aim is always to help them to learn.
6. All methods should encourage activity that demands *effort* from the children.
7. Methods should be adapted to the age and ability of the pupils.
8. Pupils should be enabled to feel that the subjects of study are related to real life and to their own lives *now*.
9. Careful preparation of each lesson. No other condition of success is more important. Even experienced teachers find such preparation necessary. Carelessness in preparation is the chief cause of failure in the classroom.
10. Good lesson notes are the foundation of good preparation.

**Observation and Practical Work**

1. Make a list of the animals or birds or flowers in your district and if possible give them each their English and vernacular names.
2. Prepare notes for a lesson, in any subject you prefer, to show how teaching should be balanced by children's activity.

**Discussion and Essays**

1. Why a teacher has to know more than he has to teach his pupils.
2. 'The attitudes of the children tend to reflect the attitudes of the teacher'. Why is this so?
3. Why is teaching-method important?
4. Discuss the view that 'the best learning is done when the teacher is not teaching'.

# XIII

# SOME WAYS OF TEACHING

The various ways of teaching children can be very broadly divided into:

*Teacher-centred methods*
and
*Child-centred methods*

In teacher-centred methods the teacher is more active than the children; in child-centred methods the children are more active than the teacher. Probably the best of all teaching is seen when these two ways are pleasantly combined.

Changing views on the nature of children have caused changes in the ways of teaching them. It is interesting to note how these changes took place in the long history of education.

### Teacher-centred Methods

1. *Class-teaching*. We are all familiar with this ancient method used 2,000 years ago in the schools of ancient Greece and Rome, and today all over the world. It is pretty certain that every reader of this book has been taught this way at some time.

The teacher takes up a prominent position in the classroom. With the blackboard behind him and his eyes on his class, he talks, and sometimes talks too much. He develops his lesson by question and answer, blackboard illustration and other visual aids. If he is a good teacher he will make the lesson a co-operative affair in which children join with both talk and chalk. He will in this way bring a 'child-centred' touch into his attitude and method. If he is a bad teacher, he will talk too much and leave the children with open mouths and empty minds, i.e. his lesson will be entirely teacher-centred.

2. *Teaching small groups.* This is really a modification of class teaching, often used to simplify the problem of teaching big classes with wide-ranges of ability. Children are divided into smaller groups and given special tasks according to their interests or ability. The teacher attends to each group in turn, giving individual help to pupils in difficulty. The advantages of this method are that children can learn at their own speed and according to their aptitude. In classes of wide age-range or ability-range it is quite essential.

*The Advantages of Class Teaching*

(a) If the teaching is good it ensures that knowledge is acquired in a systematic way.
(b) The teacher can present a topic once only instead of many times to separate groups or individuals. This is convenient and saves time.
(c) It is especially valuable in introducing new methods and procedures, e.g. in mathematics.
(d) The class method is useful for revising and co-ordinating knowledge gained by less formal methods.
(e) There is value in class discussion under the teacher's guidance when dealing with common errors and difficulties.

*The Disadvantages of Class Teaching*

(a) There is a danger that the teacher will talk too much and neglect pupil activity.
(b) Unless the class is uniform in ability either the slow or the brighter pupils may be neglected.
(c) The children are given no real social experience in this very formal class situation (see Project Method, page 84).
(d) It is extremely difficult for a teacher to maintain the interest of his class for a long period.

### Child-centred Methods

The history of how educators turned to a more child-centred view of education is interesting and helps us to understand the child-centred methods used today. It is interesting also to note that these pioneers of educational thinking and practice came from many different countries.

1. *Jean-Jacques Rousseau* (1712-1772) was a French-Swiss who rebelled against all the established ways of education. 'Do the opposite of what is usually done and you will have the right plan', he said. Here are some of his views: Your teaching must be based on the nature of children, not on what adults think they ought to know. Study your children and you will find they develop in stages. Their education must fit these stages of natural growth. Do not make them learn anything until they are ready to learn it. Train their senses first; take them into the fields and bring them into contact with natural things. Do not preach to them, but set them a good example. The teacher's job is to provide the right environment from which children will learn by solving for themselves the problems that face them. Thus Rousseau firmly established the idea of *child-centred education* which has had a great influence on teaching methods.

2. The Swiss *Heinrich Pestalozzi* (1746-1827) was a devoted follower of Rousseau. He emphasized the importance of educating children *through their senses;* through familiar things at home and in the countryside. Touch the stone, feel the water, count the windows in the classroom, measure the floor, climb the mountain, boil the kettle, see the veins of the leaf, smell the flower. Here again the teacher was to be a guide and friend who revealed to the children the ways of learning for themselves.

3. The ideas of Rousseau and Pestalozzi were put into more orderly form by the German teacher, *Friedrich Froebel* (1782-1852). His *Kindergarten* (children's garden) firmly established the child-centred method of education for young children and has influenced thousands of primary schools all over the world. The secret lies in the word *garden*. Froebel regarded each child as a *plant* with the seed of growth within him. The teacher is the *gardener* who waters and protects the plant so that it can grow into the kind of plant God intended it to be. His method was based on *play* which must be *purposeful*, not mere idle amusement. To ensure the correct kind of play he provided playthings called 'gifts' which helped the children to learn as they played. The teacher observes, guides when necessary. Froebel's ideas are still the basis of all good infant teaching today.

4. The Italian *Dr. Maria Montessori* (1870-1952) pushed the teacher still further into the background by a form of self-education. She

provided pieces of apparatus which the children could use themselves without the aid of the teacher. These were graded according to the development of the child, beginning with the education of the senses and proceeding to more complicated exercises in writing, reading and number. There were other activities, such as music and gardening and physical education, in which the children learned to live together in a happy small community. The teacher's duty was not to teach but to select the right environment. Thus the children are free to play and work as they please, but only within the conditions provided by the teacher. There are many supporters of this method for the early training of young children, but it has been criticized for not encouraging play and imagination and for relying too much on apparatus and not enough on the personal influence of the teacher.

5. *The Project Idea.* All the educational pioneers we have mentioned stressed the importance of children's activity and initiative. Then, at the end of the nineteenth century the American educator *John Dewey* (1859-1952) said individual activity was not enough. His argument was that children prepare for life by taking part in the life of the village and wider neighbourhood in which they live; that it is *social activity* that really educates children. This is a point of view that should interest African teachers, for it is important for African children to keep in close touch with the life, work and traditions of their neighbourhood.

Dewey's ideas were developed by his followers into what we usually call the *Project Method,* which is now widely used in schools all over the world. *A project* is the co-operative study of a 'real life situation' by a class, or even by a whole school, under the guidance of the teacher.

A project aims to do three things:

(a) To bring children into real contact with the activities of the school neighbourhood.
(b) To present children with 'real life' problems which they solve by thinking and working together.
(c) To develop further skills and new knowledge in school subjects while working at the project.

A project may last a whole term or may be completed in four or five weeks. An example of a project for a town school might be 'The town we live in', or 'The industries of our town'. For a country school it might be 'Farming' or 'The occupations of our village'. Suppose the chosen topic is 'Farming':

The children are divided into small groups each of which sets to work to study some aspect of farming—distribution of local crops, farming methods, farming people, farm implements and machinery, climate, transport, cash crops and crops for export, sales and marketing, the food value of farm produce and so on. As far as possible the work of the children is so planned as to include most subjects of the curriculum. In this case the obvious subjects are rural science, geography and arithmetic. But all children will have to read books, write accounts and draw diagrams. They may also make models of farm buildings and draw or paint detailed pictures of farm crops, e.g. of maize, millet, coco-bean, coffee beans and cotton boll, or of seed germination. So the arts and crafts have their opportunity also.

At the end of the project each group presents its report and the teacher attempts to bring together all the information thus produced so that the results of the project are seen as a united whole.

*The Advantages of a Project are:*
(a) It captures the enthusiasm of many children, stimulates their initiative and encourages the spirit of inquiry.
(b) Children learn to plan and co-operate with each other, which is good social training.
(c) They come into close contact with the problems of real life which they may fail to do by studying 'subjects' in school.
(d) The subjects of the curriculum are seen to be connected with real life outside the school.

*The Disadvantages are:*
(a) There is no certainty that all the children will be interested or that all of them will take a full share in the work.
(b) It is very difficult to ensure systematic progress in school subjects by this method.
(c) Some subjects of the curriculum will be neglected.
(d) The individual may be neglected by the emphasis on social activity.

*Requirements for a Successful Project*
(a) A project must be well planned by the teacher. Only teachers with really orderly minds should use this method.
(b) The children should know clearly what they have to do.
(c) At the end of the project the teacher should unite all the various contributions into a whole.

(d) The project, and each section of it, must have a clearly defined purpose easily understood.
(e) The project must fully engage the pupils' *lasting* interest.
(f) The project must be worthwhile—not merely pleasure-giving or make-believe.
(g) It must awaken curiosity and create a demand for new information.
(h) It must contain problems which the children have to solve by thinking hard.
(j) To be thoroughly successful a project should last a number of weeks—at least a month for young children, and a term for older pupils.

When we consider these advantages and disadvantages we shall probably conclude that an occasional project is a good thing, but that it should be combined with periods of formal teaching. There are several adaptations of this method. Smaller topics can be dealt with in a shorter time. The important point for teachers to note is that this is *a* method which is valuable at times but not a method for continuous use.

## Observation and Practical Work

1. Make plans for a project on any topic suitable for your district. Note carefully, (a) the headings for each study, (b) what visits are to be made, (c) books and materials to be used, (d) size of groups, (e) time to be taken.

## Discussion and Essays

1. What is meant by a 'child-centred' education?
2. Can class teaching be 'child-centred'? Give your reasons.
3. What are the advantages and disadvantages of the project method?
4. What parts of a project force pupils to think?

## XIV

## TEACHING THEM TO THINK

No matter how well we plan our teaching we shall not be educating our pupils unless we *teach them to think*. This is quite the most difficult job any teacher has to do. In very simple ways we can begin in the upper classes of the primary school. We can make sure, for example, that children give good reasons for their answers, and it is comforting to remember that when we are helping them *to understand* we are helping them to think.

In the secondary school, no real progress can be made unless our pupils acquire the habit of thinking about all they learn; and no good learning is possible without thinking. The great weakness of pupils preparing for examinations is their strong tendency to learn by committing facts to memory. Unfortunately it is sometimes possible to pass elementary examinations this way. But when such a pupil, either in school or later in his job, is asked a question requiring the capacity to think, he fails because he has not learned to think about the facts he has memorized.

The good teacher will help his pupils to combine memorizing with reasoning. Remember that in adolescence the reasoning powers are developing fast. That is why it is so sad to see so few teachers making use of this most important instrument of learning. All the time he is teaching the good teacher will insist on his pupils acquiring good work-habits; he will insist on their understanding the meaning of every word they read and every word they say. He will insist that they form their *own* conclusions rather than meekly accept the teacher's. Here are a few simple suggestions to help the keen teacher to do this successfully.

1. Encourage the expression of independent opinions, but when any pupil expresses an opinion, make him give reasons for holding it.
2. In teaching mathematics point out how reason, logic, is at work, i.e. that they are actually using their reasoning powers.
3. Teach history or geography in such a way that facts are presented to them from which certain conclusions are to be drawn. Do not draw these conclusions yourself.
4. In science lessons do not draw conclusions from experiments performed by you or the pupils. First ask the pupils to state their own conclusions, and then the class together should discuss how far they are right or wrong.
5. Encourage class discussions of social and political subjects that arise in history or civics lessons. The teacher will then criticize bad reasoning.
6. *Never* reject a thoughtful answer even if it is the wrong answer. Let the class consider it carefully and discover where the fault lies.
7. In all subjects make good use of questions that require thought, in addition to questions that require knowledge of facts.
8. Good note-making helps good thinking. (See Appendix I, p. 148).

These are just a few practical ways of helping pupils to think. They are not easy to put into practice because teachers and pupils are so anxious to 'get on with the syllabus'. But this is the only way in which our knowledge can be thoroughly digested. For knowledge is not digested until it becomes part of our mind and usable for acquiring still more knowledge. When we memorize a passage from a history book or science text-book this knowledge is not *ours*. Until we have thought about it and understood every word, it really remains in the text-book. And it is not much use to us if it stays there (see Appendix I).

# XV

# VISUAL AND AURAL AIDS

## Visual Aids and Language

Visual aids are used in schools to give meaning to words. A word-description of a terraced hillside, or of a desert or an elephant or pineapple is always made more real if we are helped by a picture of the real thing, or better still by seeing the thing itself. Hence visual aids are aids to understanding. There are for example, three ways of learning what a hippopotamus is like:

(a) by hearing it described in words as a huge grey-pink animal, weighing a ton, like a big pig with short thick legs, enormous square mouth, which lives in rivers, eats grass, etc., etc.
(b) by seeing a picture of a hippo in a river.
(c) by seeing a hippo in a river.

The third way is best; the first way is not much use; the second way is what most of us may have to rely on.

Visual aids to learning are especially important in Africa because so few children can travel far from their homes to see the world about which they have to learn. Few homes have books and pictures which children can study in their leisure time. But even more important is the fact that today African children have to begin learning a new language like English if they are to go far in their education. In this case, visual aids become essential for understanding the real meaning of many of the new words they learn, especially the nouns describing *things*.

When learning a language there is a danger that children will merely substitute a word in their own language for a word in the new language. This is the result of bad teaching. The word in the new language should immediately bring to mind a picture of the real thing, not the sound of another word. For example, if the teacher uses the word 'banana', his pupils should think of an actual banana, not of another *word* for it. This is why all modern courses in English are well illustrated with pictures. Books on geography, rural science and history also use pictures and diagrams as visual aids to understanding.

### Looking at Pictures

But this is only the beginning of our problem. Inquiry has shown that many children do not know how to look at pictures and diagrams. This is because they have not yet learnt to perceive fully what they see. They have seen the familiar scenes around their homes—goats, cattle, trees and hills—but they often do not recognize the same things in a photograph. Hence we have *to teach children how to look at pictures,* because so often they do not see what the picture has to tell. It has been observed that children who have had plenty of practice in drawing and painting understand pictures better than others.

Many children are puzzled by perspective. They may say, for example, 'What a little man!' when the picture clearly shows that the man is 'small' because he is a long way off. Children also find it difficult to see that a 'flat' picture (i.e. two dimensions) actually represents objects in three dimensions. Hence their senses have to be trained to recognize thickness, shape and distance in pictures, just as they perceive them when looking at real objects. Visual aids will not be of much use in the classroom unless teachers take care to teach children *how to observe*. This is especially true of films and film-strips, and will be still more important when television becomes a widely used visual aid. (A glance at the chapter on 'Perceiving' will help at this point.)

Visual aids are not confined to pictures in books or to brightly coloured posters of foreign lands supplied by travel agencies and commerce. There are several other aids:

*The School visit*: This provides the most real contact with the subject of study, but not necessarily the most instructive. It must be carefully planned to avoid its becoming an extra holiday.

# Visual and Aural Aids

*Films, Film-strips and Television:* Here the greatest care is needed to ensure that the children observe accurately. Apparatus is costly and requires electricity.

*Solid Objects:* These may be of two kinds, (a) objects brought into the classroom for demonstration, e.g. seeds, flowers, insects, and (b) models made by teacher and pupils to illustrate a theme in a lesson, e.g. a relief model or mathematics model.

*Flat Pictures:* Sketches, diagrams on paper or on the blackboard, maps, charts, drawings, paintings, photographs.

## The Use of Visual Aids

Visual aids are a good servant but a bad master. Here follow some principles to ensure their proper use:

*General*

1. Visual aids are not a complete method of teaching but an aid to learning.
2. Visual aids are not necessary in all lessons.
3. Too many aids in one lesson may distract attention from the main subject of the lesson.
4. Aids should be adapted to the understanding of the class.
5. Aids should be relevant to the subject of the lesson.
6. Do not use pictures when children can see and handle the real thing, e.g. in nature study, a real leaf is better than pictures of a leaf. (This is not always so: with a complex thing such as an eye, a model may well be better than a real eye).
7. Teachers and pupils should co-operate in making their own visual aids. Never give a lesson just because you have a ready-made visual aid for it, probably brought from college.
8. When possible, models should be made of local materials. Swamp clay and soil from termites' nests, mixed with water, are good for modelling. Sand, papyrus, elephant grass, bamboo, are useful for other types of model.
9. Do not leave visual aids on show for too long. When the class loses interest in them they have served their purpose.
10. Make new aids each year. This revives the teacher's interest and creates interest among the pupils.

*Blackboard, Drawings, Maps and Charts*

11. **The blackboard is the most important aid. Neatness in writing,**

printing, drawing and arrangement is essential. The pupils' note-books follow the example of the teacher's blackboard.
12. Pupils should use the blackboard.
13. All diagrams should be big, bold and simple. All lettering should be at least one inch high. Detailed maps and charts are not effective.
14. A simply drawn symbol is usually better than a realistic drawing. Children themselves draw in symbols and understand them.

*Pictures*
15. Pictures should be large.
16. Pictures do not explain themselves. Teachers should make certain that children see what the lesson requires them to see. This is best done when teachers ask questions frequently to check on the children's observation.
17. Pictures from foreign lands are often confusing because they show objects quite unfamiliar to children. Such pictures should be used with care.
18. Before the age of 13, or even later, children find it difficult to relate the details of a picture to a central idea, e.g. in a picture where the idea is to show all the work of a tea plantation, they may only see separate people doing jobs and not realize that the *whole* picture is about tea growing.

*Films and Film-strips*
19. Films should be short because attention decreases with the length of the film.
20. Pictures on film-strips should be shown slowly and with explanation. It is best not to use too many pictures in one lesson.
21. Two types of film are used in teaching. (a) Documentaries for enriching the background of history, geography, science and other lessons, (b) Teaching films proper. These actually give a series of lessons. The teacher should study the film himself before showing it to the class, so that he can guide them in their observation of it.

### Aural Aids

Visual aids appeal to the eye. Aural aids appeal to the ear. Both appeal to the understanding and are essential in teaching.

The *radio* is a valuable aid and is now widely used in schools. It is especially useful in the teaching of history, geography, civics, health-education and languages. The *record-player* and *tape-recorder* are especially useful in language teaching and musical appreciation. The tape-recorder can be used for recording folk songs and the songs children sing in school.

But the most important aural aid is the *human voice*. This is our finest musical instrument, but one that we have to learn how to play. It has a great range of tone and volume all of which should be used in the classroom. The right words spoken in the right tone of voice are the teacher's principal means of making himself understood.

### Observation and Practical Work

1. A piece of co-operation with the children: use local materials to make a relief map to include the following features: a river flowing east to west through a papyrus swamp to a lake; north there is a range of mountains, south of the river a cultivated plain.
2. Practise frequently on the blackboard. Make quite clear symbolic drawings of a cow, sheep, goat, dog, man, woman, boy, girl, tree, house, and any other things you may think useful for illustration. Try not to use more than 7 or 8 lines in each. A cow must not look like a goat, or a man like a woman.
3. Plan some simple method of explaining perspective to Class VI.

### Discussion and Essays

1. The value and danger of visual aids.
2. The use of the blackboard. Why is it usually regarded as the most important visual aid?

# XVI

# DISCIPLINE, FREEDOM AND RESPONSIBILITY

The word discipline comes from a Latin word meaning 'to learn'. From the same Latin word we get the word *disciple* which means 'one who learns from his master'. So when we think of discipline we should always remember that it is a way of *learning*. Too often we think of discipline as punishment. This is quite wrong. Discipline is a very large part of education, not a special way of keeping a class in order.

There are two kinds of discipline—external discipline and self-discipline.

*External discipline* consists of the influences that come upon us from our parents and teachers. They require us to be obedient, to be punctual, to be clean, to do our lessons and so on. They may punish us and compel us to behave properly when we misbehave. Another form of discipline that comes to us from 'outside ourselves' is our experience of getting into difficulties and finding our way out of them. This is the discipline of 'things'—we learn, for example, what we can and cannot do with fire and water and sharp tools. A most important form of external discipline is the example of a good man or the experience of seeing a brave action. All these influences that are part of external discipline come to us from the outside world of people and events. They are imposed on us; we cannot avoid them. But of course, we may refuse to learn from them.

*Self-discipline* is the control we exercise over ourselves. We might call it 'inside discipline', because it comes from the aims and desires within us. It is based on our self-respect. We exercise self-discipline when we control our temper, when we force ourselves to work although we feel lazy and even when we are controlling the ball in a game. We are self-disciplined when we are able to do the right thing without being made to do it. When children are thus able to control their desires and actions they have made great strides in growing up.

By means of external discipline the teacher should encourage self-discipline in his pupils. His demands for obedience, his encouragement in their lessons, even his punishments should always have this aim (see page 98). If this is done teachers will find that children first behave well because they are *made* to, and then begin to behave properly because they *want* to. Thus the external discipline of the teacher gradually changes into the self-discipline of his pupils. It takes a long time to acquire self-discipline but without it we are *not free* to do any of the things we want to do. We cannot fulfil any ambition without it; nor can we be successful in work or play.

This brings us to the very difficult question of *freedom*, about which many books have been written. What do we mean by saying that a person is 'free' or 'not free'? Are we free just because we are not in prison? Are we free only when we do just as we please? Are we free when we ride cheerfully on the wrong side of the road, risking death? These are questions worth answering, but not here.

In school there are two kinds of freedom we have to consider. There is the *physical freedom* of children to express themselves in play and in the occupations that help them to understand the world around them (see Chapter V). But there is also the freedom they feel *within themselves*, what we have called *freedom from frustration*. A child is not free if he is not certain of the love of his parents. He is not free when he is afraid. He is not free if he lacks confidence or is unhappy at school. He is in the prison of his fears—i.e. frustrated. Children are free when they are successfully overcoming difficulties; they are not free when faced with difficulties they cannot overcome. Freedom, then, is not just doing as we like. It is a much bigger thing. *We are free when we are able to use successfully all the abilities we possess.* And strange as it may seem, we cannot be free unless we give up some of our freedom to do as we like.

We attain this freedom by obeying rules. If we want to be free to ride a bicycle, we have to obey the rules of bodily balance i.e. the physical law of gravity. If we wish to avoid accidents we must obey the rule of the road. If we wish to be good at ball games we must keep our eye on the ball. The learning of the rules of mathematics or language are good examples from the classroom. In each case by obeying rules we have given up some freedom, and yet by giving up this freedom we have trained ourselves to use the abilities we possess.

In school quite the best way to develop self-discipline in children is to give them *responsibility*. This is much better than just telling them to be self-disciplined. Preaching does not do much good. In real life we do not even know whether we are exercising self-discipline until we have put our good intention into practice. We have not used our self-discipline to get up on a cold dark morning until we are actually out of bed. *We must act*. And giving a boy or girl a job to do forces him to act. To accept responsibility is to place ourselves in a situation where we have to say to ourselves '*It all depends on ME*.' We have to do our duty when no one is watching us. The more little jobs we can give to boys and girls in the home and at school, the more young people we have saying 'this job depends on me', the better disciplined will our school be.

Success in doing a small job makes success in a bigger job more likely. This gives confidence to boys and girls, and they become willing to discipline themselves to do bigger jobs. Thus a child may begin in Class I by being responsible for collecting the books, and finish in Class VI by taking charge of a class. This exercise of self-discipline is necessary if children are to be responsible; and in turn the experience of responsibility gives young people a wonderful opportunity to discipline themselves. When we describe anyone as a responsible person we give him very high praise. When a school has many responsible people in it, both teachers and children, it is certain to be a good school. It is only responsible people who are really grown up.

### Observation and Practical Work

1. Suppose you are in charge of Class IV. Make a list of the little jobs (responsibilities) you could give to the children during the coming week.
2. Immediately after a lesson with a class you know well, try and remember the occasions, (a) when you exerted external discipline, (b) when some pupil clearly exerted self-discipline, (c) when you exerted self-discipline.

### Discussion and Essays

'We are free when we are able to use successfully all the abilities we possess'. Discuss this statement. You are not obliged to agree with it.

Explain the connection between self-discipline and responsibility.

# XVII

# DISCIPLINE, INCENTIVES, PUNISHMENT

Rewards, encouragement, responsibility, example, punishment are all part of school discipline. All of them, if properly used, can help children to make the best of their abilities. The teacher's problem is when to use the right *incentive* (see below for definition).

There are two main causes of bad class discipline:
(a) Poor teaching.
(b) Absence of interest and incentive.

When these conditions exist children's behaviour and work will be unsatisfactory. Teachers will then use punishment of various kinds —some form of extra work, detention after school, stopping privileges, beating. For hundreds of years teachers have punished children for bad behaviour and bad work. Very few have asked the important question—'Does it work?'

### The Effects of Punishment

1. Punishment stimulates children to work for a short time but not for long periods.
2. It tends to stop bad behaviour for the moment (while the cane still hurts) but not permanently. That is to say, indiscipline is not cured but only controlled. This is important, of course.

3. It may create angry feelings against the teacher unless the pupils are sure he is 'on our side'. This is especially true of beating.

4. Punishment disturbs the class by breaking into the rhythm of learning. Again this is especially true of beating because the class are excited and turned away from their tasks.

Punishment, then, does not seem to be a really good stimulus to continued good work and behaviour. It is like the whip behind the donkey rather than the carrot in front of his nose. He will walk just fast enough to avoid the whip; but will run much faster to get the carrot. In school carrots are much more useful than whips. The carrot is an *incentive* i.e. *an encouragement to successful action*. There are many incentives to use in school.

### Incentives

1. *Success*. The most valuable incentive is confidence in the success of our efforts.
2. *Praise* is highly effective—the praise of teacher, class mates and parents. Praise has been proved to be far more effective than blame and criticism.
3. *Encouragement*. A pupil works best when he believes he can learn. Encouragement helps him to believe he *can* learn. It is especially important to encourage the slow pupils. Every little success should bring the teacher's praise and encouragement. But bright pupils need it too.
4. *Measurement of Success*. Pupils are encouraged when they see proof of their progress. It is useful for pupils to keep notes of their marks so that they can measure their own progress. A mark showing that this week John has improved on last week is a cause of much satisfaction and an incentive to do better.
5. *Setting the Right Tasks*. The success of all the above incentives depends on setting tasks the children are capable of doing. If the work is too difficult pupils will be discouraged; if it is too easy pupils will be bored and therefore ready for giving trouble.
6. *Competition* for place in class has only limited value. It affects the top half of the class only and the rest are left out of the race because they never hope to win. It tends to make pupils more interested in marks than in their subjects of study. Ask yourself: is it more important for John to know that he beat William this week in arithmetic, OR that this week John beat his own result of last week?

*Group Competition* is much better (the class divided into groups of even ability). Here pupils work for the success of the group and *all* can contribute, the gifted as well as the less gifted. Experiments have proved this to be a very effective method.

All these incentives to work well can be used together. There is no need to choose among them. When these good conditions exist the problem of classroom discipline is largely solved. For the art of preserving discipline is to remove the causes of indiscipline. When teachers ask for trouble, children always oblige. The authority of the teacher must be maintained, but maintained in such a way that friendliness prevails. But neither teachers nor children are saints, and situations will arise when punishments are necessary. If our punishments are wisely applied they play their part in helping children to achieve self-discipline.

If, then, we have to punish let us bear in mind the following principles:

1. Punishment should not be revengeful or merely to relieve angry feelings. Its aim should be to cure the offender and to increase his powers of self-discipline.
2. Never punish or blame a child because he does not understand you in class. It may be your fault.
3. Be sure the offender understands why he is being punished. Make him explain in his own words. Otherwise he may think you punish him because you do not like him.
4. Some types of punishment can be used to improve school work, e.g. 20 lines of excellent writing is worth more than 100 lines of scribble. There is no harm in acquiring knowledge and skill through punishment.
5. The certainty of mild punishment is more effective than threats of severe punishment that are not carried out. Always keep your promises.
6. To be effective punishment should be infrequent. This is especially true of beating.
7. Where teacher-pupil relationships are good, punishment will be most effective and least resented.
8. It is usually wrong to punish a whole class or school for the misconduct of a few offenders. But sometimes this is necessary in order to make everybody realize their responsibility for the good conduct of the school community.

9. If there is much punishment in your class or school, then you may be quite sure that there is something wrong, either with you, or your class, or your school, or with all three.

### Observation and Practical Work

1. Try and recall some occasions during your school-days, (a) when you were punished, (b) when you were encouraged. Which did you find the better incentive to hard work?
2. Ask an upper class to make a list of what they regard as the best incentives to hard work and to place them in order of importance. Make your own list and compare the results of both.

### Discussion and Essays

1. The advantages and disadvantages of competition as a stimulus to work.
2. The use of punishment to improve school work and behaviour.

# XVIII

# THE SCHOOL AS A COMMUNITY

A community is a group of people who are united by common purposes and common interests. A family, a village, a tribe, a nation are examples of such communities (see Chapter II). We can even speak of the world community because the nations of the world have interests in common, the greatest of which is peace. In all these different communities there is a bond that makes members of each group feel 'we belong together'.

In this book many references have been made to 'the school community'. We must now consider it in greater detail; for the school is a special kind of community in the following ways:

(a) A school is an educating community i.e. by just being part of it children receive educating influences, quite apart from the fact that they go to school to learn subjects.
(b) The school community includes teachers, children and parents.
(c) It is different from other communities because it has a much higher proportion of children to adults. Hence it cannot be organized exactly like adult communities.
(d) A school may be a machine only for teaching subjects and passing examinations. If you like this idea then there is no point in reading the rest of this chapter.
(e) A school may be a real community of lively persons, old and

young, who are preparing for real life by learning to live and work together. If you like this idea then the rest of this chapter may be helpful.

### Staff Attitudes

A good school community is one where the Head, the staff and the pupils all feel that this is *our* school, and that all have to work together to make it a better school. The most important person is the Head; not because he earns the biggest salary, but because he has the biggest responsibility. His first duty is to unite the staff into a *team*, so that all have similar views concerning the aims of the school. He has to encourage friendly attitudes among the teachers by his own co-operative and friendly attitudes to them. He will discuss school planning with them before making decisions; he will gladly receive suggestions; he will not assume that the Head has all the bright ideas. This spirit of co-operation between Head and staff is important because people are always more willing to put plans into practice if they have had a share in making them.

Similarly the Head will place real responsibilities on his staff. Preferably each member of staff should choose what he or she would like to be responsible for. They should be responsible not only for some part of the school organization e.g. games, library, craftwork, mealtimes, but also for taking charge of some hobby not necessarily related to school work. In this way teachers become more than teachers of subjects. They become friendly leaders of the children.

In their turn teachers will place responsibilities on the children. There will be smaller responsibilities in the classroom, bigger ones in the school for older children. Thus there is forged a golden chain of responsibility which goes right through the school from top to bottom, from the Head to the youngest child. The school becomes an educating community. It is a whole society instead of a lot of little pieces which do not fit into the whole plan. Individuals are all doing a job for somebody. Strange to say, boys and girls like their school best when they are willingly doing jobs for it, not when their teachers are doing jobs for them.

The following conditions will help to make this sort of community.

### School Attitudes and Organization

1. Law and order should prevail. Children do not enjoy disorder. But there should not be too many orders from Head and staff. The

Head's authority must be definite; obedience is essential. But the rule of authority should be gentle and persuasive for the life goes out of children when teachers rule with a heavy hand. Nevertheless, children should know where authority lies and learn to respect it.

2. Rules should be few. The more rules there are the more rules will be broken. When children share in the making of school rules they are more likely to obey them.

3. Responsibility should be spread as widely as possible, among the staff and among the children. The ideal would be for everybody to have a special job to do. Young children can take turns in having little duties to perform with *things;* older children, especially in secondary school, can become responsible for the welfare of small groups, e.g. as secretary of a school society.

4. Leadership should not be confined to a few chosen persons. In secondary schools there ought to be many more opportunities for leadership than those provided by prefecture and games, e.g. chairmen, treasurers and secretaries of societies, leaders of small teams doing practical jobs in and around the school.

5. The tendency of school organization should be towards co-operation rather than competition (see page 99). Class committees and school councils greatly help in the co-operation of children with staff.

6. There should be respect for the achievement of individuals. The good craftsman, needlewoman, artist, farmer or musician should receive appreciation equal to that of the good scholar, footballer or athlete. The teacher's attitude will decide whether this is so.

7. Consequently there should be ample provision for out-of-school activities and for arts and crafts and music in school. Children should experience joy in their own creations. When this happens the problems of discipline begin to fade away.

8. There should be a right attitude to work. Children should work hard. In a school community all kinds of work are necessary, therefore all kinds of job, intellectual and manual, should be equally respected. One way of encouraging this attitude is for teachers to be willing to perform with their pupils any job, clean or dirty, that has value for the community.

9. Teachers should learn more about pupils' homes, and parents should know more of the school. When teachers are welcomed at home, and parents welcomed at school, the children greatly benefit.

10. The whole school should feel itself to be part of its neighbourhood. This will happen when (a) the school helps its neighbours, (b)

the neighbours help the school, (c) parents and teachers know each other.

None of these conditions will be present in a school where teachers think of their job only as teaching the subjects of the time-table, highly important as that is. A good school community requires that teachers should have a religious attitude to life. By which I mean that they should realize that they are challenged to serve purposes greater than their own immediate comfort, and that they should have a never despairing respect for persons, especially children. The best motto for a teacher I know was written by the fourteenth century poet, Chaucer, who wrote the first modern English poetry:

*If gold rust, what shall iron do?*

The meaning of these words, written 500 years ago, is well worth an hour's discussion.

### Observation and Practical Work

1. Make two lists showing (a) the small duties that can be given to pupils in the classroom, and (b) the bigger responsibilities that can be given to older children in school.
2. Suppose you were head of a new school: plan the kind of activities you would like to introduce quite apart from school subjects needed for examinations.
3. Suggest ways in which a teacher could get to know the parents of his pupils.

### Discussion and Essays

1. What do you understand by 'the school community'?
2. What kind of person is the best kind of leader?
3. Consider ways in which your college or school might help people in its neighbourhood.

# PART V
# THE ORGANIZATION OF EDUCATION

# XIX

# THE ORGANIZATION OF SCHOOLS

In the long history of education schools are a very recent addition to mankind's efforts to educate the young. In ancient Greece and Rome schools appeared 2,000 years ago; in most parts of Europe they emerged 1,000 years later; in Africa schools have existed for about one hundred years. Schools were established because the old methods of family and tribal education were inadequate for preparing children to live in the modern world. Today education in school is essential if people are to play their part fully in modern society. Hence all countries have organized systems of education to supply needs which the old informal education in the home could not possibly provide. Gradually the elders of the tribe were replaced by trained teachers, and the teaching profession has become one of the largest and most important professions in the world. Without schools and without teachers our complex modern societies would fall into chaos in a few years. Every nation then must organize a system of schools and provide trained teachers to staff them.

## Planning for a National System

Before organizing a system of schools and colleges, a government first has to decide what its responsibilities are. As far as concerns education a government's duties are:

1. To provide equal educational opportunity for all children so that the talents of the whole nation can be used.
2. To preserve national unity by providing education for all children of whatever tribe, race or religion.
3. To develop the country's economic resources by modern technical methods and by the most efficient use of the nation's manpower.
4. To estimate what the manpower needs are and to train this manpower in its schools and colleges.

There are roughly four grades of manpower required:

Group I. This group includes doctors, lawyers, engineers, head teachers, administrators, agricultural experts, managers in industry and commerce; those who take at least a good School Certificate and go on to higher technical colleges and the university.

Group II. Includes those not in the top rank but who hold responsible positions under Group I. Some will be teachers, medical assistants, engineering, agricultural and technical assistants of all kinds, chief clerks, nurses. These will require School Certificate or an equivalent technical qualification after at least a four-year secondary course.

Group III. This is a much bigger group who will perform skilled work in agriculture, factories, workshops, building, engineering, in offices and so on. For these, secondary vocational training is necessary.

Group IV. This is the largest semi-skilled and unskilled part of the population, the basic labour force of the country. They should have at least primary education, and more when money permits. At present, many African children are deprived of even this minimum of preparation for life.

It has been estimated that to provide these manpower needs in Groups I and II, a country would have to have 5 per cent. of its children of secondary school age educated up to School Certificate. At least 20 per cent of the population are required in Group III to provide African nations with skilled technicians. An important point to note is that the more industry and machinery there is in a country, the higher must be the proportion of trained skilled workers to untrained labourers.

We are now going to examine how one particular African country might plan its educational system to fulfil these requirements. This will be better than discussing plans in general terms. For this purpose we shall study the recommendations of the Uganda Education Commission of 1963 which planned a system of national education for Uganda. The recommendations were made by an international committee after careful study of the nation's economic position and the needs of the people. As the plans involve a great expenditure of money over at least twenty years they are not likely to be out of date when this book is read.

## Plans for an African Nation

These are the recommendations in brief outline:
1. Primary education should begin at the age of 6+ and continue for 7 years i.e. the primary school age will be roughly 6+ to 13+..
2. At the end of Primary VII a proportion of pupils should be selected for admission to one of four types of secondary school.
3. Four types of secondary school:
(a) *High Schools:* These schools are of an academic type but may have a technical bias. They prepare for School and Higher Certificate and pupils will proceed to various professions, to technical colleges, teachers colleges, and to the university. The courses will be for four or six years. Age range will be 13+ to 17+ or 19+.
(b) *Technical Schools:* These schools conduct four-year courses leading to London City and Guilds examinations or their equivalent. Age range 13+ to 17+.
(c) *Farm Schools:* These schools specialize in agricultural education in four-year courses of similar standard to the above technical schools. Age range 13+ to 17+.
(d) *Secondary Schools:* These schools offer three-year courses in both general and vocational education. When finance permits the three years will be extended to four. Each school will have a bias towards some particular group of occupations for which the country needs trained recruits, for example, agriculture, engineering, and building trades, commerce and the hotel industry. The curriculum is balanced to ensure that technical skill is supported by a good general education. Age range: 13+ to 16+ or 17+.

The national system of education is, of course, completed by:
(a) Teachers Colleges,
(b) Colleges of Technology and Agriculture.
(c) The University and Medical School.

These are the bare outlines of a structure of education for an African nation. For the moment, it is left for your critical examination as we pass on to a consideration of the principles of curriculum building. But the following observations can usefully be made at this point:

The system described attempts to provide education for all types of pupil:

(a) For the ablest pupils, capable of higher college and university studies—a very small percentage, i.e. in academic Sixth Forms.
(b) For pupils of good ability, e.g. those taking School Certificate or its technical equivalent, i.e. in academic or technical or farm schools.
(c) For boys and girls of middle ability. This is a very important group who after education in the general secondary schools become the skilled producers of the nation.
(d) For the less able who have at least primary education before they commence their working lives.

## Discussion and Essays

1. Describe the system of education in your own country. How far does it cater for the four groups of occupations described on p. 108?
2. How can education be used to achieve national unity?
3. What are your country's main sources of economic wealth? How is the educational system planned to make the best use of them?

# XX

# THE CURRICULUM

When we examine the system of schools in most independent African countries, we shall find that:
1. The primary schools have the same basic education for all pupils. This is because the aim of the primary school is to lay a general foundation of knowledge and skill for use in the secondary school.
2. The curriculum of secondary schools may vary according to the vocational purpose of any particular school.

For these reasons we shall discuss the curriculum of primary and secondary schools separately. But before doing so we must explain the meaning of this rather ugly word 'curriculum'. It is a Latin word which means a 'running course', and was originally used to describe the running course of the horse chariots in the games of ancient Rome. So the *curriculum* (plural *curricula*) is the course taken by the chariot of education. In other words, it is the group of subjects chosen for pupils to study in school.

### The Essential Curriculum

School subjects must provide for the practical side of life and also for its deeper moral and spiritual aspects. To do this effectively the curriculum must satisfy the present needs of children according to the stage of their development (see Chapters IV and V). For younger children subjects will be taught simply and informally: in the more advanced stage of secondary schooling studies will be treated more formally, in greater detail and at a deeper level. But at both stages a really satisfying curriculum will include the following groups of subjects, no matter how they may be rightly disguised in the delightful activities of the primary school.

First comes *Language*, the means by which thought is transferred, either in speech or writing, from one person to another. Without language we should be as the animals, creatures of instinct only. And then *Literature*, which is language in its most beautiful form, words expressing ideas in the most telling ways. A nation's literature is a most precious heritage of its children. But great literature belongs to no one nation; it is the possession of all people who can appreciate it. Shakespeare, the great English poet and dramatist, belongs to people of all races because he described mankind in great poetry. But children will not begin with Shakespeare; their literary appreciation will begin with their traditional stories, poems and songs.

Another way in which men have employed their ability to make both useful and beautiful things is through the *arts and crafts*. This also is part of the children's heritage of beauty. Every school should provide opportunity for pupils of all ages to develop their manual skills and artistic gifts. Thus they will learn the skills of hand and eye and exercise their creative imagination. Such activities must not be regarded as useless frills, but as a necessary part of their education. *Music* and *dancing*, which children love, are also part of the experience of joy and the creation of beauty which enrich our lives (see p. 19).

No one now doubts that *science* and *mathematics* should hold an important place in the school curriculum. Both are essential for two reasons. First, they are the foundation of all technical, agricultural, industrial and economic advance, without which it would be impossible to live in the modern world. Secondly, science reveals the wonders of the physical universe in which we live; mathematics enables us to understand the art of calculation, and measurement of space and time. In the primary schools these studies will be very elementary, but they will lay a foundation for further study in later years.

*History and geography* can be considered together. *History* deals with the activities of man in the past. Its study helps us to understand *where we came from*, and therefore to understand the situation in which we now live. We have to know something of the history of our own country and how its ways of life and forms of government have come into being. In a similar way *geography* explains *where we are*. Geography deals with man's relation to his physical environment. It reveals the whole world from the countryside around the school to the farthest corners of the earth. It explains the influences of soil and climate on the lives of men and how dependent we all are on the work and products of people in other lands. Unless our pupils study geography they will never understand the world they live in.

Another essential but much neglected curriculum activity is *the education of the body*. From the earliest years children must be assisted to use their growing bodies skilfully and gracefully. Younger children will do this naturally in their games, dances and in handicrafts. Later on games are not enough but should be supplemented by scientifically planned courses of physical education aimed to develop strength and balance in bodily movement. The instructor in physical education is, then, an important member of a school staff.

Physical education will also include *health education*. In African countries, where many preventable diseases damage children's health, instruction in bodily hygiene is most important. Clearly, health education should be part of science teaching. The body is really a most exciting chemistry laboratory. When we eat or breathe or are bitten by a malarial mosquito, chemical reactions immediately begin to take place in our blood. Children, therefore, should learn the importance of clean habits and good food. And teachers and parents should realize, far more than they do at present, that hungry and unhealthy children will not be successful in school.

Finally, there is *religious education*. We can look at this most difficult part of education in two ways: first as instruction in the sacred books, beliefs and practices of a particular religion; secondly as the foundation of all moral training. Religious instruction can take place in class, and such instruction should be of the highest standard, as carefully planned for the pupils as any other school subject. But, we must remember, true religion is not only learning things about religious belief; it is also the faithful application of what we believe to the way we live. Formal teaching, necessary as it is, is not enough. The quality of a school is not finally tested in the examination room but by the behaviour of the teachers and pupils who form the school community (see Chapter XVIII). Children will learn religion from the example of the teacher's life. They will learn the meaning of honesty, helpfulness, kindness and charity when they work and play in a school where these simple qualities decide the relationships between people in school

Religion, then, is much more than a school subject; it is a way of life. To set you thinking on this idea here is a true story: After being shown round a school by the headmaster a visitor asked, 'Do you teach religion?' The headmaster replied, 'We teach nothing else'. What did he mean?

## The Primary School Curriculum

The curriculum of the primary school must cater for the needs of childhood. We must therefore try to regard the curriculum of the primary school not as a group of subjects to be learnt but as a unified experience of activity and of response to environment. If we study again the description of the needs of children in Chapter V we shall recall the meaning of 'activity' and 'response'. In that chapter we saw that children learn by being active, by seeing, touching, exploring and playing. All the time they are learning by discovering new powers in themselves and new interests and wonders in their surroundings. That is to say, they are responding to their environment. Speech, the learning of new words, is such an activity. Speech, reading and writing, are all activities that bring children into touch with people. They read stories about other children, about animals, about other countries and this widens their knowledge of the world. In this way children learn because they are interested, and because they understand what they have to learn. In other words they are learning what to them are *real* things.

In the old days, and too often even today, teaching consisted of standing in front of a class of silent children and talking and writing on a blackboard. Learning was supposed to be listening to the teacher, copying from the blackboard and learning by heart. There was little speech except the talk of the teacher; there was no movement, little physical and mental activity. This is not the way to educate children.

As we have seen, children learn best when they *want* to learn. They want to learn when they are interested. And when they are interested *they will work harder*. They will be interested when they understand what they have to learn. How then do we present the subjects of the curriculum to children in the primary school so that they will understand what they are learning? The answer is that we make the children active in *learning* what is *real* to them. Let us consider examples from some of the subjects primary schoolchildren have to learn.

Training in speech is not a mechanical chanting of words recited at the teacher's dictation, but an adventure in the use of man's most remarkable gift—the ability to express the ideas in his mind by using his tongue, lips and vocal chords. The writing of a composition, a very necessary exercise, can take the form of a description of an actual happening, a word picture produced by the imagination, a letter to a friend, an article for the class magazine, the description of a walk, of the stream or trees near the school. The point is that the subject of the composition must be *close up to* the child's experience. He must have 'been there'. Then writing ceases to become a painful exercise and is transformed into an adventure in the use of words.

Similarly mathematics must be regarded not as a book of rules or a box of tricks by means of which teachers do clever things with figures on the blackboard. It is an activity which enables children to buy and sell, to measure the desk and the classroom windows, to measure the height of trees and the width of the river. In other words, mathematics becomes another tool essential for satisfying children's desire to know more of the world around them.

Obviously the same is true of elementary science which can be taught in relation to local agriculture, their father's crops, to the hygiene of the classroom and above all to nature's wonderful machine the human body. And remember the wide scope for drawing and painting and constructing in almost all these activities. You will provide for yourselves other examples of learning by being active. This is the great need of the primary school.

Similarly history will begin with stories of the people who lived in the past. We shall begin with our own country and pass on to people in other lands. Children will learn of their own past so that they are able to realize *where they came from;* why their school and village or the neighbouring town is where it is. In geography they will begin with their school neighbourhood and then place it in the setting of their country. They will learn about rivers, plains and mountains, climate, the crops and occupations they can see around them. This knowledge will help them to understand the geography of their own country. Then they will study the geography of other countries and how dependent all countries are on other countries of the world. Both history and geography are excellent subjects for satisfying children's curiosity and sense of wonder. Field excursions, making of costumes and models, historical plays, drawing, are all activities necessary for both studies. We study our neighbourhood first because children learn best when they begin with the known and pass on to the unknown.

But let us not be misled by this emphasis on activity. We have to admit that it requires a good teacher to manage a class of forty active children! And quite apart from this need for good order, every teacher must realize that there is a place for repetition and drill that aim to create *good habits* in children. There will be the habit of attention when the teacher addresses the class (a difficult habit to learn) the habit of courtesy when listening to another person, the habit of punctuality. These are social habits. But there are also learning habits. Some habits we acquire by repetition, e.g. the twelve-times table, the spelling of a word. Writing becomes a habit after countless repetitions of certain trained movements of the hand. But the most important habit children have to learn is that of doing an uninteresting job in order to complete a bigger and more interesting task. This kind of habit children learn best by imitating unconsciously those around them who are facing the same difficulties. But sometimes it will be necessary to insist that the dull work must be done and the teacher will have to use drills and repetition for this purpose.

There is a definite place in the primary schools for formal teaching. But it is death to good primary education if teachers teach formally all the time. For even at this early stage children must begin *to think logically and imaginatively and independently*, (see our aims, page 135) and they will never do this if they spend the day learning rules and applying them mechanically.

## The Secondary Curriculum

Just as the curriculum of the primary school should provide for the needs of childhood so should the secondary curriculum cater for the needs of adolescence. Before reading further, therefore, it will be useful to re-read Chapters VI and XIV to remind ourselves what these needs are. In particular we should note that intelligence develops steadily to the end of adolescence, and that in young people of secondary school age special interests and abilities become more marked.

Before proceeding we must be quite clear what is meant by 'general education' and 'vocational education'. *General education* aims at the all round development of the pupil so that he becomes a cultured person. It should train him to think and to develop good qualities of character. It will not train a pupil for a particular job. *Vocational education* is instruction that prepares a pupil for a job, whether it be as a doctor, lawyer, teacher, farmer, motor-mechanic or carpenter.

The following are points we should bear in mind when considering the curriculum of secondary schools.
1. The aim of all education must be to produce boys and girls of good character and also productive and responsible citizens. (Refer to the two columns on page 137).
2. Boys and girls of secondary school age begin to think of their future careers and expect schools to provide for their vocational needs.
3. Secondary schools are expected to supply well trained recruits to agriculture, industry, commerce, the teaching and other professions, and to administration.
4. In African countries where development has to be carefully planned the schools have to supply these recruits in the right proportions (see page 108). The proportion of boys and girls who can have four or six years secondary education will be very small. The proportion of young people who attend the secondary schools with a vocational bias must be much larger.
5. Differences of intelligence and special abilities must be taken into account when deciding to which school a boy or girl should go.
6. Vocational education should be supported by a good general education like that outlined in the 'essential curriculum' on page 111). A mechanic who cannot read or write is not much use in a garage; an ignorant typist is not much use in an office.

The problem, then, is how to give a good vocational education and *at the same time* a good general education. This has always been a difficult problem to solve. It is not merely a question of selecting a group of vocational subjects and adding a few general subjects to support them. It is also a question of how the subjects are taught. A really good teacher can instruct his pupils in a technical subject in such a way that it helps his general education. Instruction in carpentry for instance, can become an artistic education in form and design. If we can help a boy to rejoice in the making of a perfect joint in woodwork we are contributing to his general education. If we can create enthusiasm in the production of a fine crop of maize because right methods were used to double the maize production, we have helped him to learn a new truth of science as well as to be a good farmer.

To appreciate truth is to train the mind. To build a house that not only stands up but is also beautiful to look at, is an exercise in good taste. To look happily upon neatly ploughed fields and well constructed terrace-cultivation is as good as reading a poem. The author of this book after forty years spent in the world of education, still feels he is being educated in the vocation of teaching; when he sees a young teacher managing a class of children like an artist in his profession.

The point of the above paragraph is this: general education and vocational education are not enemies; they are friends. Good vocational education can help the pupils to think, just as the study of literature and history can help pupils to think.

What we should aim at is a *balance* between the 'essential curriculum' and vocational subjects. We should also realize that several subjects of the essential curriculum are a necessary basis for vocational training.

The sciences and mathematics are the foundation for a large part of training for industry and agriculture. The arts and crafts are the basis for manual instruction. No person can go far in any occupation unless he can use his language fluently. Languages, including foreign languages, literary and historical studies are necessary for the administrative and legal professions. For the profession of teaching the 'essential curriculum' provides the necessary basis of knowledge to enable a student to specialize later in those subjects in which he is most gifted.

Thus, by carefully arranging a balance between subjects necessary for a general education and subjects necessary for vocational training, we can make a curriculum to suit the different abilities and the future careers of most pupils. In the lower classes of the secondary schools more time should be given to general education. In the higher classes more time will be given to vocational instruction. In all schools there should be provision for arts and crafts and music, some of which can take place in leisure time, especially in boarding schools. Physical education is important throughout all types of school. These principles apply equally to academic secondary schools and to vocational secondary schools. In the latter the emphasis will be placed on practical work so that the pupils are well prepared in the trades they have been learning.

### Observation and Practical Work

1. Examine a primary school time-table and calculate what proportion of time is spent on the various subjects and activities of the curriculum. Do these allotments of time satisfy your views of what a good curriculum should be?
2. Plan a curriculum, (a) for Class I in a primary school, (b) for

Class VI in a primary school, (c) for a School Certificate form in a secondary school.

### Discussion and Essays

1. What differences are there between 'activities' in a primary school and 'activities' in a secondary school?
2. What is meant by (a) the essential curriculum, and (b) a vocational education?
3. What kind of teaching is required to make a good vocational education also a good general education?
4. What is meant by 'a balanced curriculum'?

# XXI

# THE EDUCATION OF GIRLS AND CO-EDUCATION

Women are one half of mankind. And yet it is only in recent years that the education of girls has begun to receive the attention it deserves. We have to admit that the backwardness of girls' education in Africa, as in other countries, has been largely due to the belief that women are in most ways inferior to men. For thousands of years men have believed not only that the proper place for women is the home, but that homes can be managed by ignorant women. Behind this view lurks the fear that educated wives and daughters might be disobedient and neglect the children and the husband's dinner. Today other views are changing the lives of women. An educated African woman, widely experienced in the customs of many countries, recently said: 'One of the greatest battles any educator is facing in African countries is to bring about the realization that a girl is not inferior to a boy. Many women and girls have grown up to believe in and accept inferiority; many more men and boys are convinced of it.'

Several influences are steadily changing these old-fashioned attitudes. In the first place African women who have been fortunate enough to enjoy a good education have proved their abilities in several walks of life. They have successfully attended universities, they have become members of parliament and of city committees, doctors, teachers, social workers, nurses. They are also beginning to play their part in industry, commerce and public administration. Thus they have proved the case for women's education by demonstrating their usefulness outside the home. Equally important is the new desire of educated men to have educated wives as partners in the home, and educated mothers for their children. It was the great and wise African leader Dr. Aggrey, who said, 'When you educate a man, you educate an individual; but when you educate a woman you educate a family.' The result of this slow change of male attitudes to the education of women has been a steadily increasing demand for girls' education.

But we have still a long way to go. In all African countries there are far more boys than girls in the primary schools, and many of these girls leave before they have completed the primary course. In the secondary schools the proportion of girls is very small indeed. Nevertheless one of the most promising features of African education today is the new desire to educate this 'other half' of the community. The first need is to get more girls into the primary schools and to ensure that they complete the whole course. The second step is to make more provision for girls in plans for secondary education.

In planning education for girls we have to remember that while boys prepare for one career most girls have to prepare for two—for paid work before they are married and for a home career after marriage. We also have to realize that for most girls formal schooling will cease at the age of 13 or 14. For this reason it is right that even at the primary stage they should have simple training in the management of a home, in home nursing, in the preparation of food and the preservation of family health. Such instruction can quite naturally form part of elementary science and thus profitably fulfil that part of the 'essential curriculum'.

Certain aspects of girls' secondary education deserve special mention. In the first place we should note that a larger number of young women will be seeking careers outside the home. Some of these women may not wish to get married but may prefer to give their total energies to their chosen career. These women will be among the most highly educated—teachers, doctors and specialists of various kinds. On the other hand the vast majority of educated girls will spend some years in a useful career, after which they will get married, establish a home and embark upon the most important career of all. We must also remember that a very high proportion of African women will spend their lives in rural areas where knowledge of farming will always be useful.

Plans for girls' secondary education will, therefore, aim at providing a general education combined with a vocational education, and will also recognize the special role women have to play in the home. Girls in academic secondary schools should have opportunities for engaging in home-crafts and some form of artistic expression; and their science studies could well have a bias towards agricultural knowledge. The much larger group of girls, who may at present spend only three years in a secondary school with a vocational bias, can have a very interesting variety of opportunities. These schools will train girls to be typists, receptionists, caterers, nurses, dress designers and for other occupations requiring skills in which women are specially gifted. Thus, if the curriculum is carefully planned it can provide both a general and a vocational education and will ultimately add to the number of educated wives and mothers.

One further aspect of girls' education has to be mentioned. One of the good traditions of African homes has been the training of girls in modesty and good manners. This is a fine tradition which we hope will continue. But it has perhaps been influenced by the other tradition of male superiority, which has tended to weaken the self-confidence of young women when mixing with other people. For instance, African women, partly from lack of the education which gives them self-confidence, often find it difficult to take part in conversation at a party. Some are unwilling to express their opinions before men; and girls are often too shy to hold their own in a discussion with boys. Better education will remove a good deal of this lack of confidence; but girls' schools can also help by training in clear speech, discussion of current events and in confident posture when addressing other people. This is especially important for those going to be teachers.

## Co-education

Should boys and girls be educated together, or in separate schools? Most people agree that co-education is good in the primary school; but very strong disagreement exists regarding co-education in secondary schools.

The main arguments for co-education are:
1. That as brothers and sisters live together in the home boys and girls should be educated together in school.

## The Education of Girls and Co-education

2. That it is good for boys and girls to discover common interests in school work and social activities. This way they learn to respect each other as equals.
3. That when boys and girls work and play together and get to know each other, emotional strains due to differences in sex are reduced.
4. That contact with mature adults of both sexes on the school staff is good for growing boys and girls. Each sex learns to respect the other.
5. The fact that boys and girls develop emotionally and intellectually at different rates is not really important, because individual boys and girls develop at different rates from others in their own group. Any group of young people will contain members at different stages of development, whether the group is of one sex or of both sexes.
6. That it is good for boys to realize that girls can successfully compete with them intellectually.

The main arguments against co-education are these:
1. There is quite a difference between living with brothers and sisters at home and living with *other people's* brothers and sisters at school.
2. During adolescence it is quite natural for boys and girls to live separately as their interests and occupations are different. Some African communities insist on boys and girls living apart, even in the family group.
3. That competition in class between boys and girls usually results in (a) overstraining the girls who are more conscientious, and (b) girls being suppressed by the more vigorous and self-confident boys.

There is something to be said both for and against co-education. But there are also certain conditions essential to successful co-education which are not always present in African societies. The first condition is that the boys in a co-educational school should not regard girls as inferior except in physical strength. Those who support co-education would claim that co-education helps to destroy this foolish attitude to women. If this is true then this is an important argument in favour of educating boys and girls together. Another condition is that co-educational schools should contain roughly equal numbers of boys and girls. But unfortunately in the present state of girls' education this is seldom possible; girls are usually a small minority in the co-educational schools that at present exist.

In Africa, as in many other countries, the usual plan is to mix boys and girls in the primary schools and separate them in the secondary school. In universities, colleges of technology and teachers colleges women are often educated with men. As far as the education of adolescents is concerned, opinion is likely to be divided for a long time. But of one thing we can be quite certain: it matters less whether a school is co-educational or not than that it is a *good* school. The quality of a school depends less on its organization or curriculum than on the quality of the people who run it.

### Observation and Practical Work

1. Find out the number of boys and girls in (a) a primary school and (b) a mixed secondary school you know well. Work out the proportion of girls to boys. Try to give reasons for the difference.
2. Compare the number of girls in Primary I and Primary VI of two or three schools in your neighbourhood.
3. Make a list of occupations suitable for girls leaving secondary schools. What type of vocational education would each occupation require?

### Discussion and Essays

1. Why is the education of girls so important for a nation's welfare?
2. Should girls' education be different from boys'? If so, in what ways?
3. Arrange a debate on co-education.
4. What ways would you use to persuade parents to send their girls to schools and keep them there to the end of the course?

# XXII

# PROBLEMS IN PLANNING EDUCATION

No country in the world has a system of education that satisfies all its citizens. Even wealthy countries are facing difficulties in paying for all the various types of education a modern nation needs. All over the world there is a shortage of teachers because of the increasing school population. There is also the problem of selecting children from the primary schools for entry to the different types of secondary school, and also the need to guide pupils into the right jobs on leaving school. There is always the difficult task of providing equal educational opportunity for every child. These problems are very familiar to people concerned with education in African countries. But they are difficult to solve because nearly all developing countries are poor.

Here are some of the problems governments and teachers have to face:

### 1. *Compulsory Universal Primary Education*

In wealthy countries all children up to the age of 15 are compelled by law to go to school. This is called universal compulsory education. Because it is compulsory no fees are paid. The nation pays all the cost. For many African countries the cost of compulsory education is too great and free education is still a long way off. In consequence many African children do not get any schooling at all, although every effort is being made to build new schools and to train more teachers. In some countries only half the children of school age go to school.

Another obstacle to free primary education is the steady increase in the population of school age. It is estimated that the population of most African countries will have doubled between 1960 and 1990. The increase goes on steadily by between 2 per cent and 3 per cent each year. This means that it is possible to increase the total *number* of children in school each year, without increasing the *percentage* of children in a country's schools. So the difficulties facing governments are very great.

The only way of providing education for all children is to increase the wealth of the country by the hard work of its citizens and by the use of modern methods of economic production. Then there will be more money from taxation and the government will be able to spend more money on education. Everybody must realize that *the money a government spends on education is provided by taxation.*

2. *Wastage*

By wastage we mean the fall-out of children who start in Primary I but do not continue to the end of primary schooling. This is a very serious situation in Africa. The causes are various. In many cases parents are not able to continue paying the school fees, although these are usually small. Broken homes, the ignorance of parents unconvinced of the importance of education; using children to herd cattle when they ought to be at school; sickness; lack of co-operation between parents and teachers—all these influences contribute to wastage. Girls are sometimes withdrawn to attend to duties in the home; some parents withdraw girls for early marriage. As far as girls are concerned, wastage is often due to the inferior status of women whose education is not regarded as important. All wastage is not only a waste of the country's money but a wastage of children's opportunities.

3. *Promotion*

Should children be promoted each year or should they reach a certain standard of education before promotion to a higher class? It is generally agreed now that the best way is to promote each year, so that backward children may go on learning with children of their own age. This method is sometimes called automatic promotion. Some children may be backward in one subject, some in another.

This makes difficulties for the teacher. But a good teacher can arrange children in groups of similar ability so that each group can go along at its own pace. In subjects like history, geography and the arts and crafts, children of varying ability can work in the same class. Unfortunately, these methods require plenty of classroom space and plenty of books and material. These advantages seldom exist in crowded classrooms and poorly equipped schools. The difficulties are greater in small schools than in big schools. In big schools children can be more easily divided into A and B forms according to ability.

But we must not be too rigid about promotion, for schools all over Africa will have the problem of *late entry* for many years to come. There will be classes of 45, for example, with an age range of 5 to 14 years! The rate of promotion of these older children should be flexible. They have learnt many useful things out of school, their power to reason and to remember may be more developed because they are more mature, their vocabulary in their own language may be wider than that of the younger children. With such children a more individual type of promotion may be better than automatic promotion.

4. *Selection*

Good methods of selecting children to pass from primary to secondary schools are most important. To begin with we have to accept the fact that four-fifths of the population will not profit by a long period of schooling of an academic kind. But they will benefit greatly from a more practical type of education. How are we to decide which children should go to this or that type of secondary school? How do we decide *what kind* of vocational education a boy or girl should have? Our problem is not made easier when so many parents believe that their children are cleverer than their teachers know them to be. Many parents also want their children to go to the academic kind of secondary school because they think their children will get better jobs this way. In wealthy countries, not more than 15 per cent. of children go to academic secondary schools, and it will be many years before as many as 5 per cent. go to these schools in African countries.

One way of solving these problems is to have all types of education in one big secondary school to which all children go, and gradually select children within the school for different types of schooling. This requires huge schools of 2,000 children. In the big cities of the United States there are schools of 5,000 or 6,000. But this arrangement is only possible (a) when there is compulsory education up to 15 or

16 and (b) when there is a population of hundreds of thousands near the school. In Africa these conditions seldom exist.

Many western countries use intelligence and attainment tests and primary school records for selection. On the whole these tests have proved very useful for this purpose; but parents and teachers are still not satisfied with the results. As we noted in Chapter VII tests of intelligence and attainment are being worked out for use in African schools. When reliable tests have been constructed the best way to select children for secondary education will be to combine, (a) *intelligence tests* (which indicate how intelligent a child is apart from what he knows), (b) *attainment tests* (which indicate the standard a child has attained in certain essential subjects like language and number), and (c) the *school record* (which is the teacher's opinion of a pupil's progress and character).

Both parents and teachers must realize that equal educational opportunity for all does not mean the *same* education for all, but that all children should have the *right kind* of education. In Great Britain this principle has been stated thus: Every child shall have an education *suited to his ability and aptitudes*. What selection has to do is to discover what a child's abilities are, and then place him in the right school for developing them.

### 5. *Vocational Guidance*

We must not only provide vocational education but also help children to enter suitable occupations. We must remember that square pegs do not fit into round holes. Nothing is more discouraging than that a young person should feel that he is in the wrong job. It would, therefore, be a splendid thing if governments and schools could provide careers advisers to guide boys and girls into the right jobs. This is already being done in some African countries; but much more could be done. Obviously advice on careers would be based on the intelligence and special aptitudes of school leavers as revealed in tests and the school record. The school record will show not only whether a boy is intelligent, but also whether he is industrious, honest, persevering, possessed of initiative, and of reliable character. For getting a job these qualities are most important.

### 6. *The Supply of Teachers*

All over the world there is a shortage of teachers. This is due to the desire of all peoples to educate their children, and to the steady increase in population, and also to teachers leaving their profession on marriage or for better paid jobs. Education is impossible without teachers. Schools can be built in a few months; but it takes three or four years to train a teacher after he has already had several years of secondary education. So any government that wants to develop its schools has to look a long way ahead to provide teachers for them. We cannot get more teachers until the secondary schools produce more entrants to the teachers' colleges and universities; and this will not happen until there are more secondary schools. We shall discuss this problem again in paragraph 8.

## 7. Paying for Education

The money for the maintenance of our schools and colleges comes from several sources: most of it comes from local and national taxation, some comes from fees, some from the contributions of religious bodies, and, at present, quite large sums may come from wealthier nations and educational foundations overseas. This last source of money will not go on for ever. Quite soon African countries will have to rely entirely on their own national income, which, of course, they would prefer to be able to do.

The peoples and governments of independent African countries have astonished the world by their determination to provide education for their children. They have been willing to spend as much as 25-30 per cent. of their national budgets on education, which very few nations do. But if a country's total national income is small, the amount spent on education will be small too. The only way to get more money for this purpose is to produce more wealth so that citizens can be taxed more heavily.

Fortunately countries all over the world regard money spent on education as a good *investment* for the future. Well educated citizens will produce more wealth. But if this investment is to bring good results the following conditions must be satisfied:

(a) The right kinds of education must be provided and in the right proportions.
(b) The right number of students should be provided for each type of education.
(c) The right kind of teacher and equipment must be provided for the schools and colleges.
(d) There should be opportunities for immediate employment on leaving school or college.

(e) Training in the most modern methods of agricultural and industrial production should be provided.
(f) The most economical balance of manpower requirements should be planned.

## 8. *What should come first?*

The governments and peoples of developing countries have very difficult choices to make when planning their systems of education. There is seldom enough money to develop all parts of the system at the same time. A nation has also to provide money for the cost of its government and civil service, for hospitals, roads, electrical schemes, water supply, agriculture and industry. So education can only have a share of the money available from taxation. But apart from this we cannot have schools without teachers; and teachers take several years to produce. They cannot be produced unless secondary schools send students to the training colleges and universities. And teachers' colleges must also have highly educated lecturers to prepare their students for the schools. Thus a system of education is like a chain, each link of which is an essential part of the chain. If one link is missing the chain is useless; if one link is too small and weak the chain will soon break after a little use.

Another decision governments have to make is whether to have a little education for all and neglect higher education for the few able to profit by advanced learning. What would happen then? Another choice might be to concentrate on educating the 5 per cent. ablest students and neglect the great body of the nation's children. What would happen then? Another decision might be to spend all the money on technical education. What would happen then? These are all questions you can decide for yourselves in discussion. But be sure you first collect all the facts!

Instead of giving ready-made solutions, I am going to put before you an actual situation in an African country which is typical of the conditions existing in most parts of Africa. Here are the facts:

1. The population is about eight million; 90 per cent. work on the land; the soil and climate are good; industry must be developed; there is water power for electricity; more roads are needed. The population is increasing rapidly.

2. Only 50 per cent. of the children go to primary school; about 10 per cent. to vocational secondary school, and 2 per cent. to academic

secondary schools. In the primary schools there is a good deal of wastage, especially among girls.
3. There is a good University and a good College of Technology.
4. There is a great shortage of teachers for all kinds of school, both primary and secondary. About one-third of the teachers are untrained and poorly educated.
5. Many teachers are leaving the schools to go into the civil service where pay is better.
6. About 70 per cent of the population are illiterate.

Suppose you were the Minister for Education what would you decide to do? In making your choice bear in mind:
1. That secondary schools depend on primary schools.
2. That teachers' training colleges depend on secondary schools.
3. That universities depend on advanced studies in academic secondary schools.
4. That all schools depend on a good supply of well trained teachers.
5. That girls make good teachers as well as men.
6. That teachers in technical and agricultural schools require special training.
7. That a nation needs highly educated men and women in the top ranks of the civil service and other professions.
8. That national wealth is created by well trained workers.
9. That it is a bad thing for any nation when a high proportion of its adult population cannot read or write.
10. That some improvements can be made quickly and without great expense, e.g. providing text books and school materials. That some improvements may be made in one year; some in five years; some may take ten years. That schools can be built in one or two years, but teachers must be trained for three or four years.
11. That the big decision you have to make is what should come first, then second, then third. That is, you have to decide on *priorities*.

### Observation and Practical Work

1. Try and discover the main causes of 'wastage' in your area (at home or near college).
2. Find out how your local government pays for education in your home area.
3. Examine the methods of selection for secondary education in your area and suggest how they might be improved.
4. If you lived in a country where only 15 per cent. of children go to

school, what factors would you have to bear in mind in order to raise the proportion to 80 per cent in twenty years?

### Discussion and Essays

1. What conditions are necessary for establishing free compulsory education in any country?
2. If you were Minister for Education how would you deal with the shortage of teachers in your country?
3. Methods of promotion.
4. What is vocational guidance?

# PART VI

# AIMS AND IDEALS

# XXIII

## THE AIMS OF EDUCATION FOR TODAY

There is no better general definition of the aim of education than the ancient African belief that *education is a preparation for life* (see page 16). By this definition we think of education as a preparation for every part of living: for the satisfaction of our material needs, for the growth of our personal talents as well as for the formation of our personality and character. This definition also requires us to think of education as a preparation for loyal service in our local and national communities. It thus includes the claims of the individual person and also the claims of society. Here then is a firm foundation on which to base more detailed discussion.

The history of education during the last 2,000 years has shown that people change their aims in education *when their view of God and man change* and when their *social needs change*. Today views about God and man are different from what they were a hundred years ago; and social and economic changes are taking place every day. So, when in Africa today we say that education is a preparation for life, we have also to ask

(a) For what kind of life are we to prepare?
(b) For what kind of individual are we to prepare?
1. *For what kind of life?* A brief answer to this question would be: for the best kind of life that we can live in Africa today. We prepare,

then, for living a good life in new African countries where ways of life are changing, new ways are being tested, and some old ways are disappearing. We prepare for life in the villages and in the towns, on the farms and in workshops, factories and offices, in schools and churches, in local and national government.

We are aware that life in our new countries offers young people opportunities and also faces them with dangers. There are opportunities for valuable service to our community; and also glittering prizes for clever and selfish men. There is the danger of more wealth for the wealthy and greater poverty for the poor. There are the bitter feelings between races and tribes to be removed, for these delay our progress towards national unity. There is the need that all citizens should respect the law, which is the first need of a new nation. In the humble life of the village, in commerce and in the courts of our rulers, there is a call for responsible and honest men. We aim at a kind of society where there are jobs for all and responsibility for all.

2. *For what kind of individual are we to prepare?* No teachers pretend that they send forth a finished product into the world. That we can never hope to do. All we can do is to set our children on the way. Even so, we remember with sadness the thousands who get too little education. But when we feel depressed on saying good-bye to children who ought to stay longer at school, we should recall the words of the great Greek teacher Plato, written over 2,000 years ago and still true: 'The beginning, you know, is always the most important part, especially when you are dealing with anything young and tender. That is the time when character is being moulded and easily takes any impress one may wish to stamp on it.' So, if we are going to set children on the right road we must make a good job of their early education and ask what skills, attitudes and qualities of character we should aim to produce in our schools. Here follow some of the answers.

### Answers for our Schools

1. The establishment of literacy—reading, writing, good speech and the foundations of number. These are the basic skills that make possible communication between man and man.
2. Knowledge and skill that lay the foundations for earning a living. These are the tools of the producer.
3. The fullest development of personality through the fullest use of the natural gifts of intellect, manual and artistic skill and the cultivation of the human body through play.

4. Training in independent, logical and imaginative thinking.
5. The provision of social experience that enables children to live and work easily with others.
6. The development of self-discipline that enables children to control unworthy desires and to strengthen worthy ambitions.
7. Training in the use of responsibility as a preparation for citizenship in village, town and nation; especially in personal responsibility for being honest and incorruptible in both private and public affairs.
8. Helping children to think as citizens of a national community by learning respect for other tribes and races.
9. The preservation of the best customs and traditions of their country.

These aims represent a tremendous task for teachers. But they point the way we should be going, which is the important thing. It is our job to get as far along that road as we can.

### The Individual and the Community

You may have noted that in the above list about half the aims refer to the personal development of individuals and about half to the claims of the community. Some people believe that we have to choose between education that puts the individual first and education which puts the community first. Let us examine these views.

1. *The individual first*. This view maintains that the development of individuals is more important than the claims of society. Concentrate on making good persons, because nothing good enters human society except through the lives of men and women. In the practice of education supporters of this view emphasize the *present needs* of children, the cultivation of their individual gifts, self-expression, the encouragement of original ideas. They would sometimes leave the choice of subjects to the pupils. They would not emphasize external discipline but would depend on experience in school to develop self-discipline. Briefly, they say, education is to make a man.

Critics of this view maintain that such education will not make the right kind of man, that it will create selfish individuals who care little for their social responsibilities.

2. *The community comes first*. According to this view of education children should be trained only to serve the nation, even if this interferes with their individual development. School subjects would be selected to serve the economic needs of the community. There would be a tendency to shape the ideas of young people to a single pattern so

## The Aims of Education for Today

that they would all think alike. External discipline would be strict; the emphasis would be on producing a future citizen of a certain type, not on the present needs and development of individual children. The ideal citizen would be one who obeys rather than one who thinks, and one whose self-disciplines were dependent on a few well learned rules of conduct.

Critics of this view say that citizens should not all think alike because society needs men and women of different opinions if it is to be vigorous and healthy.

Clearly, there is value in each point of view. We have, then, to ask an interesting question: Is it possible to have a form of education which *at the same time* develops individual personality and also produces good citizens? Can we avoid the dangers of each type of education? Have we really got to choose between producing a good person and producing a good citizen? Surely we can have both if we avoid the extremes of each kind of education.

We may find an answer to our question if we compare side by side the qualities we should expect to find in a well educated man with those we require in a man who is to play a full part in his community.

| I<br>*Individual Needs* | II<br>*Society's Needs* |
|---|---|
| 1. Physical health | 1. Healthy citizens |
| 2. Useful knowledge and skills | 2. Productive workers |
| 3. Good social qualities | 3. Co-operative citizens |
| 4. Development of special talents | 4. Specialists in art, science and technology |
| 5. Power to think logically and independently | 5. Thoughtful citizens, teachers, lawyers, politicians, administrators. Citizens unafraid to express their opinions. |
| 6. Creative imagination | 6. Development of new ideas in the arts, government and industry. |
| 7. Self-confidence | 7. Leaders with a sense of responsibility |
| 8. Sound character | 8. Honest, courageous, responsible, industrious citizens. |

Do not these two columns suggest that it is possible to plan our education so that no individual needs are neglected and the nation gets the good citizens it requires? It must surely be evident that a good person and a good member of society are the same thing. Without the qualities of personality in the first column we shall never supply the needs of society outlined in the second column. The truth is that *just as good people help to make a good society, so does a good society help to make good people* (see Chapter XVIII).

### Aims and Personal Belief

Every teacher has to decide for himself what his aims are to be. His choice will depend on what he believes about God, Man and material things. Too few of us teachers realize that what we believe determines what we teach and how we teach. There are three questions we all have to answer if we are to discover what our aims really are:

Who am I?
Where am I?
Where ought I to be going?

1. *Who am I?* We might answer thus:

I am not only a thing of flesh, blood, bone and nerves that can be explained by chemistry; I am also a spiritual being with a mind and a soul. As a child of God I feel myself to be related to other men as brothers. The Bantu proverb which says 'Man is other Men' explains why I have a duty of service, respect and love towards them. I do not believe that material possessions are the most important things in life, nor do I wish to pursue them at the expense of other people. I know I am capable of pursuing unselfish aims, although I also know that I shall often fail in generosity, because I am human. As far as I can see, this view of myself belongs to the best part of African tradition. And as I want to be a teacher, my aim must be to help children to grow up so that they become vital personalities and good citizens. Education is not just passing examinations and learning useful facts.

*OR*, we may answer:

All I know for sure about myself is that I've a body to feed and a pocket to fill. I have got to look after myself because no one else will. The things that count in this life are money and the power that money gives. I believe in myself. I love my family, but I am not interested in the welfare of other people. They must look after themselves. Life is a struggle and the weak get left behind. My view of education is that children should be taught only useful subjects that help them to make their way in a competitive world. Occupations like music and the arts and school societies are a waste of time.

2. *Where am I?* One answer might be:

I am living in an African country whose future depends partly on me and my work. We are poor; great efforts are required to increase our national wealth so that the life of the people can be improved by schools and hospitals and other social services. I must join in these efforts for moral and material improvement.

My pupils face strong temptations, for there are many material rewards for clever and dishonest men who know how to exploit the poor and the foolish. If I am what I say I am, all my efforts as a teacher should aim to produce men and women whose sense of social responsibility guides their ambitions and conduct.

*OR* another answer might be:

I am living in a new African country full of good chances for getting wealth and power. If I use my brains and keep my eyes open my chance will come. I don't intend to be left behind. Why let your life be governed by moral principle? No one will thank you for it. So I intend to make personal profit out of 'Where I am'.

3. *Where ought I to be going?*

This question has already been answered by both of our imaginary teachers. When a man has decided who he is, and where he is, he has already decided where he is going. Each of them has chosen his aims in life and therefore his aims for education. For in the end it is not ideas from a book that decide what our aims in education shall be; it is *what we believe and what we are* that finally decides.

\* \* \* \*

I am aware that at this moment I am writing the last paragraph of this book. And I am wondering whether it is possible for me to summarize in one brief phrase all I have been trying to say. We have discovered that education is a long and difficult journey in which imperfect teachers try to help imperfect children along a slippery road. In the classroom, in and out of school and by our example, we shall do our best to show the way. What then am I asking you to do? I think all the time I have been saying to teachers:

*Help children to grow up by giving them jobs to do.*

Should any reader think this definition of education to be too simple, then I suspect he is not using his imagination.

If, then, on your retirement, either into old age or into the Inspectorate, only one former pupil should come to you and say, 'Sir, (Miss), you helped me to grow up', then you will have received your reward.

### Observation and Practical Work

1. In your vacation inquire of older people, especially grandparents, around your home and ask them how they were taught when children. Try and discover in what ways their education was 'a preparation for life'.
2. Examine carefully the suggestions for the aims of education in this chapter and (a) decide whether you agree and (b) add any aims you think have been omitted.

### Discussion and Essays

1. What do you think are the most important aims for education in your country today?
2. 'Children should be taught only useful subjects that help them to earn a living'. Explain why you agree or disagree with this statement.
3. 'Good people help to make a good society and a good society helps to make good people'. Explain the meaning of this statement and give examples of how this happens.
4. What do we mean when we say 'What we believe decides how we teach'?

# APPENDIX I

## HOW TO STUDY

It is the object of this appendix to suggest ways of study that will help students in training not only to acquire good work-habits themselves but to help their pupils to do the same. What is said in the following pages is especially important for those between the ages of fifteen and twenty-five, for these are the years when attitudes to work begin to settle firmly into our personality and determine the quality of our mental life.

### Making Knowledge our Own

We have already seen that our intelligence is largely decided at birth. No amount of hard work will turn a stupid man into a genius. Nevertheless, although our intellectual gifts are determined by our ancestors, the extent to which we use them is decided largely by ourselves. We cannot increase our brain power; but we can all make far better use of the brains we have. These facts are not as discouraging as they may seem. If we have only an average intelligence, which is true of most of us, we can nevertheless make the best use of it; if we are more intelligent we can make a finer instrument of our mind if we consciously acquire correct methods of learning. Too few people use the brains they possess in the right way or to their full capacity. A good teacher will make full use of his intellectual gifts and help his pupils to do the same.

The most desirable intellectual habit to form is that of making knowledge *our own*. The most dangerous habit to acquire during these years is that of slipping into the lazy way of preserving knowledge and ideas in other people's words. That is not an educated man who retains undigested paragraphs of a text-book in his memory and turns on the flow of words just as he memorized them, without adding an idea of his own. Everything he says is second-hand and in the truest sense, thought-less. He has not thought about the facts or meanings the words are intended to convey. He has not assimilated his reading, he has contributed nothing of his own experience and has failed to relate what he has read with the knowledge he already possesses. Briefly, he has not made this knowledge his own; in effect it stays in the text-book.

The assimilation of knowledge can well be compared with digestion. We take in food and then the organs of the body perform the complicated chemical processes involved in nutrition, until our food is transformed into the physical energy by which we live. The food has been digested and assimilated, i.e. absorbed. *It is part of us.* To be effective all learning should undergo similar processes if what we learn is to become part of ourselves. If we persist in using other people's words, the words and phrasing of the books we read, we shall fail to develop this essential habit of making knowledge our own. Just as our digestion suffers when we swallow unchewed chunks of food, so our minds suffer when presented with undigested facts, which have not been subjected to the critical *thinking that relates what we are learning to the knowledge we already possess.*

When knowledge is well digested it becomes part of our personality. All the knowledge we get from books and teachers becomes part of all our thinking rather than isolated bits of information unrelated to each other. When what we have learned becomes first-hand rather than second-hand knowledge, then we can begin to think. We produce our own ideas, we become responsible for our own learning, and we *learn at an increasing speed* because the mind is working as it was intended to work. Briefly, we are training ourselves to think creatively. If, then, we would make the best use of our minds we must learn to strengthen them by using them honestly and strenuously during working hours. To use the minds of other men while thinking we are using our own is a most dangerous form of self-deception.

The following pages are intended to help students in a practical way to make the best use of the brains they possess.

### Memory and Remembering

Memory, like intelligence, is basically an innate quality of the mind and may be simply defined as the capacity to retain the facts of past experience. These facts may have been encountered in the reading of books or in our contacts with people and things. Although people differ in their capacity to remember most of us have quite good memories. But to describe memory in this way is to over-simplify the problem; for what we too easily regard as a general memory, is in fact a group of separate memories each of which tends to become specialized in remembering special groups of facts. For example, we may be good or bad at remembering faces or words or figures or music or historical events, but not necessarily good at remembering all these things equally well.

Specialization in memory is very important when we come to ask the question: 'Can we improve our memory?' If we mean by this question 'Can we by certain exercises turn a bad memory into a good one?' the answer is 'No.' (So do not waste your money on courses in 'Memory Training'.) We cannot, for instance, improve our memory for faces or historical events by learning passages of poetry by heart. All we do in this case is to improve our capacity to learn poetry by heart; which is a useful accomplishment. Thus practice in memorizing a particular type of material does not improve our general capacity to remember; but it does increase our capacity to memorize that particular type of material. And also, by proving that we can memorize one type of material, it encourages us to realize that we may be able to memorize other types of material just as easily.

Hence when we ask whether we can improve our memory we are really asking the wrong question. The question we ought to ask is: *'Can we improve our Remembering?'* The answer is, 'We can.'

Remembering is a much more important process than memorizing. Remembering involves learning and understanding; memorizing is merely mechanical repetition and may become an obstacle to true learning, because it fails to encourage the practice of thinking about the new knowledge that confronts us in each stage of learning. Hence students with only moderately good memories should be encouraged. It is far more important to have an average intelligence and memory than it is to have a good memory without intelligence. Some of the most stupid men have excellent memories but they are not of much use to society. An intelligent man in a good library is likely to be a far more effective student and citizen than an unintelligent man with a good memory. The reason is that *thinking and remembering are inseparable;* they are both part of the complex activity of learning, which involves feeling, observing, remembering, selecting, understanding, reasoning, all gathered together in the human activity we call WORK.

All that has been said in this section is especially important for those who are forced to study in a foreign language. In these circumstances, especially where a wide range of subjects is involved, there is a great temptation to learn long passages by heart without full understanding of what is learnt. Here exists a serious obstacle to any form of learning beyond the elementary stages. Memorizing takes the place of understanding, with the result that knowledge is not assimilated *and the acquisition of new knowledge becomes increasingly difficult*.

But it is wrong to think that all memorizing is useless. Memorizing can play a useful part in learning if the right types of learning material are memorized. There are certain facts we must have at our fingers' ends as tools for further learning. A good example of such tools are arithmetic tables. We cannot do arithmetic unless we know without hesitation that, for example, $7 \times 8 = 56$. So we must learn our tables by heart. Other examples are formulae in mathematics and all branches of science, and, to a lesser degree, dates in history, if we are to acquire a feeling for the chronology of historical events.

### Learning and Remembering

There are several principles or conditions involved in good learning and remembering:

1. Good remembering requires good learning.
2. We must approach all learning activities in an attitude of confidence, quietly feeling sure that we are going to understand, and remember.
3. We must be interested in what we are learning.

To achieve this interest is not always easy, for study often includes what seems to be dull and pointless drudgery. Where the task in hand is distasteful there must be a deliberate effort of attention, which is best gained by seeking for a satisfying *motive* for the task. We must become conscious of a personal need for the material we are studying, which means that we must see the *end* for which we are working. It may be an immediate or a long distant aim; for example, to pass an examination next term or to excel in our career. When we are clear about the reason for working we gradually acquire the right *feeling* for study and this provides us with the emotional drive to press on. We are *well motivated*.

4. The more we learn well the more are we able to learn. This is so because new knowledge is built upon knowledge we already possess. When our present knowledge is well arranged in our minds and in our note-books we are better able to relate what we are learning with what we have already learned. This is because our mind will receive and retain new facts and ideas more readily when the new facts and ideas are linked with facts and ideas already in the mind.

5. Remembering and learning depend upon thinking and understanding. We cannot remember what we do not understand (although we may be able to memorize it); nor can we understand anything without thinking about it. There is no point in memorizing words we do not understand, because we cannot use them accurately. Hence we have to think about the meaning of words if we are to understand them and use them. For instance, to grasp the meaning of this paragraph, the reader must know quite clearly what the writer means by such words as remembering, memorizing, thinking, and understanding. Otherwise the reader will not know what the writer is trying to say, no matter how well he learns the whole paragraph by heart.

6. Learning and remembering involve *observation*. We must observe carefully the nature of the material we have to learn; for this will decide the method we should use in order to learn it well.

7. Learning and remembering involve repetition and *testing*. Repetition of facts to be learnt is less important than testing. When we think we have learned a piece of work we must test ourselves to discover whether we really know it. More will be said later concerning this aspect of learning.

We shall find all these principles operating in the following practical hints for effective learning.

### Hints for Effective Learning

The following advice will be valuable for all teachers and students who wish to improve their own methods of study and is likely to help them to assist their older pupils towards acquiring better ways of learning. When, for instance, a pupil of secondary school age has presented a good piece of work the teacher can ask him how he set about it, thus making him aware of the value of good methods of preparation, and suggesting others. Similarly, the pupil who produces a bad piece of work can be made conscious of the wrong methods used and better ways can be suggested. Students who honestly practise habits of working on the lines suggested will find their ability to learn greatly increased.

1. *Put your body in the attitude of work*. Be comfortable, but not too comfortable; sit in an upright chair at a table or desk, not in a lounging position. The arm-chair must be reserved for the joys of reading for pleasure when serious work is over.

2. *Have pen or pencil and paper* at hand and a good light to read or write in. Remember that physical effort involving slight muscular tension, such as is required when using a pen for the writing of notes or drawing diagrams, helps us to remember. This is because we cannot write sense without a good deal of concentration on what we are writing, and concentration is essential to good learning.

3. *Learn in wholes and not in parts*. This advice refers especially to pieces of poetry or fine prose to be committed to memory. Do not learn 'two lines at a time' but read through the whole passage slowly several times until the whole is familiar. Strange as it may seem, you will not only learn the passage more quickly but you will retain it in your memory for a longer period of time. If the passage is long it can be divided into several 'wholes'.

4. *Grasp the meaning* of any passage or chapter in a book. If it is a poem to be learnt by heart, for instance, first determine the main ideas, facts or pictures the poet wishes to convey. Note significant or unusual words and the general theme. If it is a chapter of a literary or historical nature, first grasp the general contents by reading it straight through. Note relationships of ideas, the order of facts, key situations which lead to other situations and events. Then read again more slowly, striving to make the words and phrases bring a *feeling of nearness* to the people and events which are being described. Try and throw *yourself* into the events described so that you seem to take part in them.

You have not understood a sentence until each word has meaning for you. It will not help your understanding to learn difficult passages by heart if you don't know what the words mean. It is at this point that we begin to get dishonest with ourselves. Lazy readers are apt to pass over a difficult passage which, when made clear to them by a strenuous attempt to get at its meaning, may make all the difference between remembering and forgetting.

5. *Space your learning*. This principle applies to most types of learning but particularly to material that is to be learned by heart. We can learn more quickly and remember what we have learnt for a longer

period if we learn intensively for several short periods than if we try to learn our lesson in one big effort.

For instance, suppose on Monday you are set twenty lines of poetry, or a vocabulary or a group of chemical formulae to learn by Wednesday, you will learn most effectively if you spend five minutes on Monday evening, five minutes on Tuesday and five minutes on Wednesday morning, and an additional three minutes on each occasion to test yourself, than if you devoted a continuous half-hour on Tuesday evening to complete the task in one effort.

(N.B. The next two paragraphs are especially important for revision.)

6. *Test yourself.* Testing what we think we have learned is of the utmost importance. Testing enables us to know what we know, and also to know what we do not know. Self-testing is an essential stage in learning. The next paragraph suggests how you should test yourself.

7. *Appeal to hand and eye* while you are learning and testing. You are not working and you are not learning when you are staring at a page of print in the vague hope that a few odd facts will stay in your mind. You should be *doing* things most of the time. Use pencil and paper, make notes (in your own words), draw rough maps and diagrams. If you find it helps you, recite important phrases quietly to yourself so that you just hear your own whisper. Test yourself *not by verbal recitation but by writing* so that you may *see* the results of your self-testing. Draw maps and diagrams *from memory* to discover if you have the right shapes and proportions in your mind's eye. Thus you will see the results of your efforts staring you honestly and accusingly in the face.

A good example of learning in this way is the drawing of a piece of science apparatus to illustrate an experiment. You will not learn much by gazing at the diagram in the text-book. The first thing to realize is that you are representing *activity*, e.g. chemical activity. Your diagram has to work. Too many students draw beautiful diagrams that would not work in practice because they omit some essential piece of apparatus. This indicates that they have not understood the processes going on in the apparatus. Hence when drawing the diagram from memory the test is not how beautiful but how accurate it is, how workable. And this means that in the drawing of it the student must *think his way step by step through his diagram*, fully aware of what is happening in each section of the apparatus.

It will have been noted that this advice to appeal to hand and eye and to use pencil and paper fulfils the condition that helps concentration. The writer of this book could not write these words he is now writing without concentrating on what he wants to say. We are bound to concentrate when we put words or pictures on paper. This is a far more effective means of concentrating than saying to oneself: 'I am not concentrating; I really must concentrate.' Our mind will soon be flying away from the book unless it is absorbingly interesting.

8. *Be honest with yourself.* Do not believe you are working when you are gazing at the printed page or merely copying other people's words into a note-book. This is a dangerous form of self-deception. You are not working if you are not thinking. Any fool can copy other people's words and ideas; the good student turns them to his own use by thinking about them.

9. *Do not work when tired*—but be sure you are really tired. Sitting for too long may easily give the impression of exhaustion, when in fact all that is needed is more oxygen in the blood stream. To remedy this take some exercise and fresh air.

10. Finally, before settling down to work, decide whether the type of study you are to prepare for is the type that requires spaced learning or the type that demands a long drive of work involving prolonged application e.g. literary or historical reading, essay writing, problems in mathematics or science. These last types of study are dealt with more fully later (see *The Student in Action*, page 150).

## How to Make Notes

Note-making is a valuable aid to learning and a useful mental exercise. We shall not make good notes unless we realize that everyone has two vocabularies. The first is the vocabulary we use when we speak or write, which is our *active* vocabulary: the second is the much more extensive vocabulary of words we understand when reading a book but do not habitually use in our own speech or writing. This is our *passive* vocabulary. Each vocabulary increases as we learn the meaning of more words in the process of our reading and education, for our active vocabulary is fed from the less used passive vocabulary. However large or small our active vocabulary may be, the point to note about it is that it is *our own*, and it is gradually extended only to the extent that we understand the full meaning of the words we add to it. This last fact is very important for making notes.

The following are suggestions for good note-making.

1. Notes can be made in two ways: *either* by copying selected sentences from the book we are reading *or* by making brief notes in our own words. The first way is wrong; the second way is right. In the first case we are not thinking, therefore we shall forget; in the second we are thinking and therefore we shall remember.

2. Orderly notes result from orderly thinking, and orderly thinking results in remembering. Therefore our notes should develop in logical order. We should restrict our notes to key facts and ideas, briefly stated but clearly phrased, in our own words.

3. We should appeal to our visual memory by visible orderliness and arrangement, emphasized by an economical system of underlining. There is a danger in underlining. We may underline too much and then the whole purpose of headings and sub-headings is lost.

4. Briefly noted examples, telling quotations, should be recorded to bring key facts and ideas to our notice both in the first study and in revision. Older students should acquire the habit of making cross-references to other parts of the book and to other books. This is most valuable and a proof of thoughtful reading. It works like this: as we are reading, we may remember a passage in another book which is clearly related to the subject matter of our notes. Refer to this passage in the notes. Again, if, as we read, interpretations of our own enter our thoughts, we should make a brief note of them. When this happens we can be quite sure we are thinking for ourselves, which is a main purpose of any study.

5. When rough notes have been taken at lectures, these should be neatly recorded and expanded *as soon as possible* after the lecture. This is most important for revision later.

6. Use abbreviations and invent them for your own convenience. These become a useful form of short-hand.

7. It is useful to leave the left-hand page of a note-book blank for additional notes and illustrations (if paper is in good supply).

8. Tidy notes are essential for effective revision. But beware of wasting too much time on artistic underlinings. Extravagant use of coloured inks usually suggests an empty mind.

9. Finally, the system of note-making we employ should be our own invention, evolved out of our own experience of the way we learn and remember best. Nevertheless it should follow the general lines suggested here.

## The Student in Action

A student is often set a piece of work to do which involves a long period of concentrated effort. It may be an essay, a piece of elementary research in history or a broad topic in science. How shall we achieve the best results?

For over half a century psychologists have been examining the processes that seem to take place in the minds of distinguished poets, philosophers, and scientists when producing their best work. They have concluded that there is a general similarity in these mental processes that is related to the creative work of more ordinary minds. One British philosopher and psychologist has simplified the situation by suggesting that there are five stages in creative thinking (and we can all be creative thinkers in a small way even in writing an essay). To these stages he gives the following long names:

        Preparation
        Incubation
        Intimation
        Illumination
        Verification

1. *Preparation:* This is the stage of reading, note-making and re-reading, of piling up a heap of facts related and unrelated, of feeling muddled and lost, despairing and momentarily hopeful, of seeing no end and no meaning in the disorderly pile that has been born out of our industry.

Muddled as it may seem, this stage is of great importance. Without it nothing good can happen. This is the stage when we glue ourselves to our desk and stick there till we can do no more, working faithfully and making our heap of facts.

Then stop.

2. *Incubation:* It is usually best at this point to drop the work altogether. Relax. Play a game, go for a walk, dance, chat, enjoy some music. Above all try and arrange for at least one night's sleep before you continue with the task.

For the mind is strangely and wonderfully made; on the condition, but only on this condition, that we have done the preliminary work, the mind will do a good deal of quiet work for us while we play and sleep. Slowly we find ourselves emerging from the muddle left by our preparation; the mind will begin to 'incubate' the general plan for which we are seeking. We can compare the mind to a cloakroom in which the coats have been put on the wrong pegs; and during the night there comes a good angel who sorts them out and puts them on the right pegs. The cloakroom is in better order in the morning. Thus our ideas are taking orderly shape through no conscious effort of ours.

3. *Intimation:* While this sorting out is going on we may find, as we go about our daily affairs, that ideas emerge on the edge of our consciousness that seem to be relevant to our problem. We may experience that tantalising sensation when we say 'It is on the tip of my tongue'. These are the *intimations* that suggest our theme is taking shape. But all will not be clear. We have now to do some hard thinking, greatly helped if we begin to arrange our notes into a sensible order of headings. This sorting out is essential to the next stage.

4. *Illumination:* Clearly or dimly the plan begins to emerge; quickly or slowly the solution comes.

The time for renewed work has arrived. Again we place ourselves in the attitude of work, arrange our notes and then begin to write. The quality of what we write will depend on the thoroughness of our *preparation*, and our capacity to bring some original ideas into our thinking. When we have produced one new idea of our own we are beginning to create.

5. *Verification:* But we have not finished. After the Almighty had created the heavens and the earth he 'saw that it was good'. Only then did he rest on his sabbath. We must do likewise. We must test our conclusions, verify our facts, to make sure that we have said what we wanted to say. Some of our bright ideas may appear to be not so bright after all; some of our sentences may not make sense; our spelling and punctuation may require attention. When we have faithfully made sure 'that it is good,' we can sit back and say with many great men: The loveliest thing in the world is work—when it is over.

# APPENDIX II

## GLOSSARY OF EDUCATIONAL TERMS

*Activity:* as applied to education, the free and constructive movements of children fully employed on a task, imposed or self-imposed. It is to be contrasted with the passive nature of class-teaching, where only the teacher is active.

*Adapt:* to fit into the circumstances in which one lives, e.g. in school or village or changing customs.

*Adolescence:* the period in human development between the end of childhood and the beginning of adulthood, i.e. roughly ages 13 to 18 or 20.

*Aptitude:* natural ability to acquire special types of knowledge or skill. (See *Tests*.)

*Attention:* the concentration of the whole personality on a particular activity or interest. (See page 61.)

*Character:* the group of habits, attitudes of mind, moral outlook, and ideals that together distinguish one person from another. (See Chapter VIII.)

*Childhood:* the period in a person's development between infancy and adolescence.

*Chronological age:* the age of a person calculated from the time of his birth. (See *Mental Age*.)

*Co-education:* the education of boys and girls in the same school and in the same classes.

*Community:* a group of persons with common interests, e.g. family, village, school, town, nation.

*Concept:* a pattern of ideas that gives a general idea of an object or word. (See page 63.)

*Co-operation:* the activity of a group of persons working together for a definite purpose.

*Culture:* the language, arts, artistic and scientific achievements, social customs, beliefs of a people or country, *considered as one whole.*

*Curriculum:* the subjects of study in a school.

*Discipline:* the essential element of discipline in education is the idea of *control*. This control may come from other people, e.g. parents and teachers, and also from circumstances that limit our freedom. This is *external discipline*. It may also come from a person's own aims, desires and self-respect; this is *self-discipline*. (See Chapter XVI.)

*Drive:* an inborn tendency urging an animal or human being towards the achievement of a definite end. (See page 25.)

*Emotion:* strong feeling created by the activity of an *innate tendency*.

*Endowment:* in education refers to the inborn capacities of human beings, e.g. intelligence, memory, special aptitudes.

*Environment:* literally 'that which surrounds'. In education refers to the physical, social and moral conditions in which children live. (See Chapters I, II and III.)

*Freedom:* has several meanings in education; (a) the unrestricted activity of children in work and play, (b) the absence of obstacles to the satisfaction of a desire or the performance of a task, i.e. the absence of *frustration*, (c) the absence of fear or repression which prevent normal mental development. (See Chapters XVI and XVII.)

*Frustration:* the situation where children are prevented from satisfying their needs because of physical or emotional obstacles they cannot overcome. The chief causes of frustration are fear, a sense of insecurity and lack of ability or opportunity to achieve conscious aims. (See page 95.)

*Heredity:* the passing on from parents to children of physical and mental qualities such as physical appearance (e.g. 'he is like his father') and intelligence.

*Heritage:* what has been inherited from past generations (a) in people by *heredity*, (b) in society the customs, traditions, language, arts and religious beliefs.

*Ideal:* a long-term aim, guided by our best motives, towards which we strive. (See page 54.)

*Identification:* the situation where a person imagines himself to be another person whom he admires. (See page 33.)

*Imagination:* the capacity to form mental images, (a) of past experiences and also (b) to construct new patterns of thought out of past experiences. (See page 66.)

*Imaging:* the creation of mental pictures or images of past events. (See page 66.)

*Imitation:* following the example of another; performing an action as seen performed by another. (See page 32.)

*Impulse:* the tendency to act immediately, without thinking, after an emotional stimulus.

*Inborn:* see *Innate*.

*Incentive:* encouragement to further endeavour. (See page 99.)

*Infancy:* the stage of human development between birth and childhood. It usually refers to the first two years of life but educationally the term is applied to a much longer period, even up to 7 years.

*Innate:* literally means *inborn,* i.e. present in the individual at birth, e.g. we say intelligence is *innate*. (See page 25.)

*Innate tendency:* inborn urge or drive. (See page 24 and Chapter V.)

*Instinct:* a source of energy in animals which impels them to behave in a fixed pattern following a certain stimulus, e.g. nest-making instinct of birds. (See page 24.)

*Intelligence:* the innate capacity to grasp relationships between facts and between ideas. The ability to reason. There is no good simple definition. (See page 46.)

*Intelligence tests:* tests which measure intelligence. (See page 46.)

*Intelligence Quotient:* (I.Q.): (See *Mental Age,* and also page 47.)

*Interest:* the feeling of 'worthwhileness' experienced by a person in any activity that excites his attention. It is very important in all learning and teaching because (a) it assists learning by stimulating attention and (b) it is one of the results of good teaching as much as it is a cause of good learning. (See page 61.)

*Kinaesthetic:* a word which describes the sense of movement and position of various parts of the body. (See page 24.)

*Manipulation:* the handling of objects; in education especially those involving manual skills.

*Maturity:* the fullest development of a human being. The process of this development is called *maturation*. (See page 42.)

*Mental Age:* the age of a child measured by his intelligence as distinct from his *chronological age* which is measured from the date of his birth. Mental age is often recorded by an *Intelligence Quotient* (I.Q.) which is obtained by the formula given on page 47.

*Motive:* an influence which helps a person to act in order to achieve a purpose. An *incentive*. Hence we get the verb to motivate, which means to provide an incentive; and *motivation* which describes the situation where the incentive is working.

*Perception:* the process of becoming aware of objects or situations around us. (See Chapter IX.)

*Personality:* the physical, mental, moral and social qualities of an individual, including both inherited and acquired characteristics, that together make him the sort of person he is. (See Chapter VIII.)

*Play:* activity for its own sake, whether physical or mental. In education we are especially concerned with the play of children. (See page 35.)

*Principles:* as applied to education, the basic ideas that form the foundations of educational theory and practice.

*Psychologist:* one whose profession it is to study human personality. The educational psychologist applies psychology to the study of children's behaviour, to problems of intelligence and the processes of learning and teaching.

*Psychology:* the study of human personality and behaviour.

*Record-card:* a card used in schools for recording the progress and behaviour of each pupil.

*Reflex Action:* the automatic response to a stimulus, e.g. breathing, sneezing. A *conditioned reflex* is a response that has been learned by experience, e.g. fear of loud noises or of fire. (See page 23.)

*Response:* a feeling or action resulting from a stimulus from another person or from a situation which faces a person, e.g. the response to good teaching would probably be an attentive class.

*Responsibility:* the fact or feeling of obligation to perform a duty. (See Chapters XVI, XVII, XVIII.)

*Self-assertion:* the situation where a person insists on his own rights.

*Self-centred:* a person is *self*-centred when he thinks only of his own interests.

*Self-control:* the situation where a person exercises control over his own feelings and actions.

*Self-development:* development or growth of a person due to innate capacity to grow up and also to that person's own efforts.

*Senses:* (See the 'six senses' described on page 24.)

*Society:* a group of individuals living together and sharing common interests e.g. village society, school society. (See also *Community*.)

*Stimulus:* an influence that arouses a person to activity. e.g. encouragement or punishment may stimulate effort in study. (From a Latin word for a pointed stick or *goad*.)

*Suggestibility:* readiness to accept a *suggestion*. A *suggestible* person is one who easily accepts a suggestion without being aware that he is doing so. Suggestion is very important in education. (See p. 33.)

*Temperament:* the physical and emotional qualities of an individual that affect his behaviour. (See page 44.)

*Tests:* a type of examination given to a group or to an individual to measure certain qualities and abilities. In schools the most important tests are:
   (a) *Intelligence tests:* which measure innate intelligence as distinct from knowledge acquired by education.
   (b) *Attainment tests:* which measure a child's attainment in particular subjects e.g. arithmetic, language.
   (c) *Aptitude tests:* which measure a person's natural ability in special types of knowledge and skill e.g. mathematical, space relations, mechanical skill.
   (d) *Vocational aptitude tests:* determine a person's suitability for a particular occupation. (See Chapter VII.)

*Tradition:* laws, customs, beliefs, folk stories passed down from one generation to another.

*Urge:* (See *Drive* and page 25.)

*Vocational education:* education planned to train pupils for their future career in different types of occupation. (See Chapter XX.)

*Will:* the conscious impulse which involves the whole personality in a decision to act in a particular way. Will has been described as 'character in action'.

# INDEX

Activity, 31, 114-6
Adaptation, 11, 12-5, 16-20, 27
Adolescence, 33, 39-43, 116
Age: chronological, 47
   mental, 47
Aggression, 31, 40
Agriculture, 11, 12, 17, 18, 117, 118
Aims, 1, 16-20, 22, 26, 27, 134-9
Anger, 30, 31, 40
Aptitudes, 40, 48-50, 70, 116, 128
Arts, 19, 20, 41, 49, 104, 112, 115, 118, 122
Attainment test, 128
Attention, 59, 61, 62, 116
Attitudes, 74-9, 103-5, 120
Aural aids, 92
Authority, 42, 103-4

Belief, 5, 136-9

Change, social, 8, 10-15
Character, 51-4, 117, 135-7
Child-centred education, 22, 81-6
Childhood, 29-38, 39, 126
Citizenship, 134-9
Co-education, 122-4
Collecting, 34
Community, 7-14, 102-5, 136-8
Competition, 99, 104, 123
Compulsory education, 125
Concept, 63-5
Construction, 34, 42
Co-operation, 53, 104
Crafts, 18, 19, 103, 104, 112, 115, 117, 122
Curiosity, 33
Curriculum, 40, 111-8
Custom, 8, 39, 53, 120-1

Dancing, 20, 112, 113
Dewey, J., 84
Discipline, 54, 94-6, 98-101, 104, 136, 137
Drama, 68, 115
Drive, see 'Innate tendency'

Education: compulsory, 125
   general, 116-8, 122
   primary, 109, 114-6
   secondary, 109, 116-8
   vocational, 109, 116-8, 122, 130
Emotion, 27, 30, 34, 36, 37, 40, 123
Encouragement, 42, 45, 53, 78, 99

Environment 1, 2, 3-5, 7-14, 27, 53, 77, 104, 126, 135
Example, 8, 9, 43, 75, 77, 83, 94, 98

Family, 3, 7-10, 17
Fear, 30, 31, 95
Food, 9, 10, 113
Forgetting, 70-2
Freedom, 19, 35, 36, 40, 43, 95-6, 104, 136
Froebel, 83
Frustration, 30, 37, 41, 95

Girls' education, 120-4
Group learning, 82, 100
Growing points, 22-7, 37
Growth, 22

Habits, 24, 53, 116
Health education, 113
Heredity, 2, 3, 45, 52
Hobbies, 103, 104
Home, 3, 7-10, 17, 27, 35, 104, 121, 122

Ideals, 5, 17, 41, 54, 134-9
Identification, 33
Imaging, 66-8
Imagination, 66-9, 136, 137
Imitation, 32, 33
Incentive, 99-101
Independence, 40, 41
Individual differences, 44-50
Innate tendency, 24-5, 29-38
Instinct, 24-5
Intelligence, 25-6, 29, 40, 46-8, 50, 115
Intelligence quotient, 47
Intelligence tests, 46-8, 128
Interest, 60, 61, 76, 80, 85, 86, 98

Kinaesthetic sense, 24, 67
Kindergarten, 83
Kwashiorkor, 9

Language, 10-13, 61, 64, 89, 90
Leadership, 41, 103-5
Learning, 57-61, 63-9
Learning readiness, 50
Loyalties, 41

Manpower, 108, 117
Manual skills, see 'Arts' and 'Crafts'
Maturity, 42-3

Memory, 57, 70-2
Method, 79-80, 81-6, 88, 90-3
Montessori, 83
Motive, 98-101
Music, 18, 19, 20, 112

Nation, 3, 7, 10, 12, 13, 107-10, 125-31, 135-8
Nature, 23-6
Neighbourhood, 9, 10, 14, 18, 19, 104, 115
Nursery schools, 37

Obedience, 33, 53, 94, 95, 104
Observation, 58, 60, 89-92
Organization, 102-5, 107-10, 111-18

Parents, 5, 8, 9, 13, 16, 17, 31, 32, 34, 35, 37, 40, 41, 52, 53, 105, 121
Perception, 57-62
Personality, 2, 51-4, 75-7, 35, 137
Pestalozzi, 83
Pictures, 90-2
Play, 35-7, 83, 84, 135
Priorities, 130-1
Problem solving, 65, 66
Projects, 84-6
Promotion, 126
Punishment, 94, 98-101
Purpose, 4, 5, 26-7, 29, 54, 134-9

Reasoning, 65, 66, 87-8
Record card, 128
Reflex action, 23
Reflex, conditioned, 23
Religious education, 42, 105, 113
Remembering, 70-2
Repetition, 71
Response, 27, 114
Responsibility, 40, 42, 43, 95, 96, 103, 104, 105, 136, 139
Rewards, 98
Ridicule, 42
Rousseau, J. J., 83
Rules, 104

Science, 10-12, 20, see 'Curriculum'
Security, emotional, 30-2, 52
Selection, 127
Self-assertion, 31
Self-centred, 32
Self-control, 40, 41, 43, 52, 95
Self-development, 35
Self-submission, 32
Senses, 24, 59, 60, 67, 83, 84
Society, 7, 8, 10-14, 108, 120-1, 134-9
Speech, 62, 78, 93, 114
Staff, 74-80, 103, 104
Stimulus, 58, 59, 61, 98, 99
Suggestibility, 33

Teachers, 4, 5, 7, 8, 13, 14, 16, 17-20, 22, 27, 29, 32, 35, 36, 41, 43, 66, 74-80, 103-5, 128, 131, 138-9
Teaching, 18, 19, 50, 61, 62, 67-9, 70, 79-80, 81-6, 87-8, 89-93, 98, 114, 116
Temperament, 44-6
Thinking, 63-8, 87-8, 136
Toys, 34-7
Tribe, 3, 7, 12, 14, 16-7, 18

Urge, see 'Innate Tendency'

Visual aids, 89-92
Vocational guidance, 128

Wastage, 126
Wholeness, 54
Will, 32
Work, 104

Published by Oxford University Press, Eastern Africa Branch, P.O. Box 72532, Science House, Monrovia Street, Nairobi and printed by Acme Press (K) Ltd., P.O. Box 40497, Mfangano Street, Nairobi, on paper manufactured by Panafrican Paper Mills, P.O. Box 535, Webuye, Kenya.